Napoleon's Captivity in Relation to Sir Hudson Lowe

R C Seaton

BIBLIOLIFE

NAPOLEON'S CAPTIVITY

IN RELATION TO

SIR HUDSON LOWE

BY

R. C. SEATON, M.A.

LATE FELLOW OF JESUS COLLEGE, CAMBRIDGE; AUTHOR OF
" SIR HUDSON LOWE AND NAPOLEON "

LONDON

GEORGE BELL AND SONS

1903

CHISWICK PRESS: CHARLES WHITTINGHAM AND CO.
TOOKS COURT, CHANCERY LANE, LONDON.

PREFACE

A S my small book, "Sir Hudson Lowe and Napoleon," published in 1898, has now been for some
time out of print, I have thought it better to rewrite
it, incorporating any new matter that might be necessary to bring the subject up to date. This is therefore
practically a new book dealing with the same subject
as the previous volume.

I have derived much information about the earlier
life of Sir Hudson Lowe from the proof-sheets of Sir
Harris Nicolas—kindly lent me by Miss Lowe—for his
intended "History of the Captivity." After the pre-
mature death of Sir Harris Nicolas, whose care and
accuracy are well known, the sheets were used to some
extent by Mr. Forsyth. I am encouraged to write
again by the revival of interest in the St. Helena controversy which has followed the publication of Lord
Rosebery's "Napoleon: the Last Phase."

The portrait of Sir Hudson Lowe is from a pencil
drawing by Wyvill, in the possession of Miss Lowe,
made in 1832. This is the only authentic portrait in
existence.

PREFACE

Some of the names in the map of St. Helena are taken from a map of the island published in 1816 by Lieut. R. P. Read, in the possession of my friend Dr. J. Frederick W. Silk, whom I here thank for his kind permission to use it.

ERRATUM

Page 18, line 7, *for* " is " *read* " was."

CONTENTS

ILLUSTRATIONS

NAPOLEON

AND

SIR HUDSON LOWE

CHAPTER I

THE PROBLEM STATED

Character of Napoleon a perpetual subject of controversy.—
Why Sir Hudson Lowe's character has not been cleared.—
Recent literature on the subject.—Forsyth, the foreign Com-
missioners, Jackson, Lady Malcolm, Lord Rosebery, Stokoe,
Sloane, Watson, Rose, French and German writers.

THE character and career of Napoleon form a
subject of perennial interest. He is already one
of those personages about whom, after all is said, the
most diverse opinions are held because their names
have become identified with principles that go down
to the roots of character and conduct. In the struggle
between Caesar and the Senate (for Pompeius never
counted as a statesman), who shall say which side
was right? People take part, and will continue to
take part, with one side or the other according to
their temperament and training, but not as the result
of argument. Few Catholics will condemn Mary of
Scotland, few Protestants will defend her. The char-

acter of Cromwell, again, will always be a subject of dispute. New facts may come forth in abundance, but each man will interpret them according to his previously formed opinions. So it is with Napoleon. Whatever his merits as a military leader, he was essentially a politician, for when he said of himself *je suis tout à fait un être politique* he spoke the exact truth.

While the French Revolution started the new system of *la carrière ouverte aux talents*, it was Napoleon that consolidated that system and surrounded it with the glamour of military glory. Hence his name will always be the watchword of those who think that each man should have a fair chance in the world—"equality of opportunity," as it is called—and that the artificial inequalities of birth and rank should no longer usurp the power due only to the inequality of nature. Another class of people will always be attracted by the personality of Napoleon, which offers so many facets to the student of humanity. There is, then, no wonder that we never come to an end of Napoleon, and that every new book only furnishes matter for fresh controversy.

No apology therefore is necessary for an attempt to clear the character of one whose name is indissolubly connected with the closing scenes of the Emperor's life, of one who has been so maligned that his name has become a byword for peevishness of temper, coarseness of language, and petty persecution. It is scarcely necessary to say that I refer to

Sir Hudson Lowe, the Governor of St. Helena during Napoleon's captivity. French national pride has made it a point of patriotism to cling to charges long after they have been disproved, but something different might have been expected from ourselves.

A writer who attempts to defend one whom a large body of opinion—I will not say public opinion—has condemned must expect to be charged with what is commonly called "whitewashing"—an odious name for an odious thing—and I have not escaped. Sir Hudson Lowe has, however, no need of "whitewashing," for he makes no demand on our generosity. It is only necessary to clear away the mud that has been so persistently thrown at him.

Soon after the death of Napoleon, a small but noisy group, aided by political interest, party spite, and the specious statements of a lying book, captured the ear of the public with their version of the treatment of the Emperor at St. Helena, and they have more or less kept it ever since. A few months before the death of Sir Hudson Lowe, Colonel Basil Jackson thus expressed himself in the "United Service Magazine":[1] "So complete a reaction has taken place, in this country at least, that it may now be doubted whether any man of information and reflection can be found to countenance opinions unfavourable to Sir Hudson Lowe." There are, however, a good many such to be found even now. No man, it is true, " of information

[1] "U. S. Mag.," Oct., 1843.

and reflection " ought to entertain such opinions, but there is considerable excuse to be made for the British public. When people have once had it instilled into their mind that atrocious deeds have been done, they do not rest content (and all honour to them for the feeling) till they have seen punishment inflicted for the wrongdoing. But they are not always so careful about securing the real culprit. If they can offer up some one as an expiatory sacrifice their virtue is only too apt to be satisfied. Thus we read in Greek history of the alarm and suspicion caused by the mutilation of the Hermae at Athens when the perpetrators of the outrage could not be discovered. One of the accused, Thucydides tells us, thought it better to confess with a promise of impunity and give information against others in order to make the State cease from its suspicion. " By this course, though it was doubtful whether those who suffered had been punished justly or not, yet the rest of the community were manifestly benefited." [1] So in the more modern days of the " Popish Plot " many were condemned without evidence worthy of the name merely to appease the fears of the people. The most recent example is furnished by the Dreyfus case, in which it was seriously contended by many—quite apart from the guilt or innocence of the accused— that it was better for an innocent man to suffer than for the whole country to be kept in agitation. Some-

[1] Thuc., vi. 60.

thing like this happened in judging of the treatment of Napoleon at St. Helena. It was first admitted without sufficient ground that Napoleon had been ill-used, and then, finding it was possible to make a victim of Sir Hudson Lowe, the outraged public promptly sent him into the wilderness to bear the sins of the British Government, whatever they may have been.

There is little similarity between Sir Hudson Lowe and Lord Byron, yet they have this in common, that both, though for very different reasons, have been made scapegoats to save the character of the nation. Byron was offered up to vindicate our domestic virtue, Sir Hudson Lowe to expiate our supposed sins against Napoleon. There is also the difference that Byron was guilty, while Sir Hudson Lowe was innocent; but of both the remark of Macaulay on Byron holds good: " He is a sort of whipping-boy, by whose vicarious agonies all the other transgressors of the same class are, it is supposed, sufficiently chastised. . . . At length our anger is satisfied. Our victim is ruined and heart-broken. And our virtue goes quietly to sleep for seven years more." The literature of the day, and more especially that of France, became so saturated with the notion of Napoleon as a victim to the petty male-volence of his so-called " jailer " and " executioner " that people at last accepted the story as unquestioned truth. And they had the good excuse that Sir Hudson Lowe himself had never spoken out when he might have done so with effect—a fatal mistake for which he paid the penalty to the day of his death. The reason why he thus acted will be dealt with later on. It was not till the publication of the " History of the Captivity of Napoleon at St. Helena," by the late Mr. William Forsyth, Q.C., nine years after the death of Sir Hudson Lowe, that a full statement was made on the other side, or even that it became widely known that there was another side. His character is there completely vindicated, it is true, but it is also completely buried. It is unreasonable to expect the average reader to work his way through three thick volumes weighted with numerous official documents. The materials are only too ample, the vindication is only too complete. And yet Forsyth's book is slight compared with what would have been the production of Sir Harris Nicolas (had he lived longer), to whom the Lowe papers were in the first instance intrusted. His plan had been to print almost every letter and document at full length in chronological order, connecting them with explanatory remarks. This would have resulted, as Forsyth says, in a work of eight or nine closely printed octavo volumes, which, if only from the cost, must have been inaccessible to the general public : " moreover," he adds, " the interest of the subject was suffocated under a mass of minute detail, which would have bewildered the attention and exhausted the patience of the reader." [1]

In a less degree the same criticism may be passed

[1] Preface, p. viii.

upon Forsyth's own book, for the three volumes, though excellently written, are rather a storehouse from which the necessary proofs may be drawn than a readable and available defence of Sir Hudson Lowe. What was wanted was a book setting out the salient facts in reasonable compass. It is true the book has made a certain impression on the public. It is no longer possible to speak of Sir Hudson Lowe with the same licence of abuse as was heard previously; but, while it is allowed that " he was not a bad man," he is still charged with harshness of temper, want of courtesy, violence of language and vacillation of purpose. But, if Forsyth's book had made the impression that it ought to have made, it would have been hardly worth while for a respectable firm to have republished, even with certain omissions and corrections, O'Meara's " Voice from St. Helena." It may be admitted that the Governor was occasionally wanting in tact and judgement, but with that exception the charges that are still made against him show either that certain writers have not read Forsyth's book with sufficient care, or that they have closed their eyes to the plainest evidence.

In spite of his limitations Sir Hudson Lowe was a man of a thoroughly kind heart, and any ungenerous treatment of Napoleon cannot fairly be charged upon him, no, nor even upon a Government in a normal state, but upon a Government suffering, in common with the British nation and the rest of Europe, from a severe attack of nerves. Napoleon had shaken all the thrones of Europe—that of Great Britain less than others, it is true; still, the British Government *was* affected, and it had not sufficient confidence in itself to show much generosity.

Fifty years ago Mr. Forsyth wrote: " The historian has charged him [Sir Hudson Lowe] with meanness and cruelty, and the satirist has turned him into ridicule. He has been painted as a man whose conduct and language befitted the turnkey of a gaol rather than a British officer intrusted with the execution of a duty of unparalleled delicacy and importance. And even those who have duly estimated the difficulty of his task, and suspected the veracity of his assailants, have been unable to divest themselves of an uneasy consciousness that he might have performed his duty in a more gracious manner. The tone of their defence has been rather that of apology than vindication. And for this I cannot but think that Sir Hudson has himself been in some degree to blame. When we consider the ample materials he possessed for refuting his enemies and putting the libellers to shame, we cannot but marvel that he should have allowed the grave to close over him without having published his defence to the world."

Since then many books have appeared on the subject of Napoleon at St. Helena, among them the

[1] " History of the Captivity of Napoleon at St. Helena," i. 122, 123.

separate accounts of the three foreign Commissioners —first-hand evidence of much importance—but the words above quoted are almost as true now as when they were written, so difficult, so almost impossible is it to eradicate deep-seated prejudice from the public mind.[1] An honourable exception must be made in favour of the writer of the notice on Sir Hudson Lowe in the "Dictionary of National Biography," who has done justice to the good intentions and excellent performance of duty by the Governor of St. Helena.

One French writer—Lamartine—has had the good sense and moral courage to run counter to the prepossessions of his fellow-countrymen in the following remarkable words: " In reading with attention the correspondence and notes exchanged on every pretext between the attendants on Napoleon and Sir Hudson Lowe, one is confounded at the insults, the provocations, and the invectives with which the captive and his friends outraged the Governor at every turn. Napoleon at that time sought to excite by cries of pain the pity of the English Parliament, and to furnish a grievance to the speakers of the opposition against the Ministry, in order to obtain a removal nearer to

[1] The interesting and valuable evidence of Colonel Basil Jackson in his little book, " Notes and Reminiscences of a Staff Officer relating to Waterloo and St. Helena" (1877), was only printed for private circulation, and so has been little known hitherto. It has lately been published by Mr. Murray (1903).

Europe. The desire of provoking insult by insult, and of afterwards exhibiting these insults as crimes to the indignation of the Continent, is plainly evident in all these letters." [1] To this must be added the review of Forsyth's book in the " Revue des Deux Mondes " [2] by M. de Viel-Castel, in which the writer frankly states that his preconceived opinion of Sir Hudson Lowe has been quite changed by Forsyth's defence. Of this change he says: " I have not myself arrived at it without having to surmount the repugnance which every sincere and serious mind experiences in renouncing any long-cherished conviction." Such an experience is apt to produce a " laceration of mind " (as Johnson well calls it) to which no one submits if he can help it.

Most of the above was written six years ago. Since then interest has greatly revived in St. Helena matters owing to various publications. First in time and in importance as regards the personal relations between Napoleon and Sir Hudson Lowe comes " Lady Malcolm's Diary of St. Helena in 1816 and 1817," published in 1899, which is also the diary of Admiral Sir Pulteney Malcolm, for much of it was taken down from his dictation. Sir Pulteney Malcolm was for a year the Admiral on the station, having arrived at St. Helena in June, 1816. In this position he was independent of the Governor's authority and so could

---

[1] " Histoire de la Restauration," vi. 416.

[2] 1855, vol. ix. pp. 292 foll.

visit Longwood without his permission. The editor of the " Diary," Sir Arthur Wilson, very truly says in his introduction:

" There is nothing in this record that lends any support to the grave charges once made against Sir Hudson Lowe, but which have long since been refuted. Indeed, if further disproof of these charges were needed it would be found here. But the diary does bring out in somewhat strong relief the less attractive side of Sir Hudson's character and the defects of his method of rule. It is clear that Sir Pulteney Malcolm found Sir Hudson Lowe a difficult person to deal with, and that before they finally parted the relations between the two men were greatly strained."

At this time Sir Hudson Lowe was no doubt somewhat difficult to get on with, but the strained relations between the two officers give additional weight to the Admiral's testimony to the Governor's dignified behaviour at his last interview with Napoleon in August, 1816. There is no mystery about these strained relations. After this last interview the Admiral refrained from visiting Longwood for some time to show his disapproval of Napoleon's conduct to the Governor, but as he was about to sail for the Cape towards the end of September, he though it proper before his departure to pay a final visit of ceremony. Sir Hudson did not altogether approve of the intended visit, on the ground that it might be interpreted as a condonation of Napoleon's behaviour. On the other hand the Admiral argued that if he did not go it would be said that he had been influenced by the Governor. It seems probable that the Admiral was right, but it was a point on which two gentlemen might reasonably hold different opinions. Finally, Sir Hudson withdrew his objection and the visit was paid. After the Admiral's return from the Cape a more serious difference between the Governor and himself arose respecting the transports and supplies of the island, which led to a disagreeable correspondence, but this had nothing to do with Napoleon. The Admiral also thought that there was a system of spying, but this will be dealt with later on.

The next book is Lord Rosebery's "Napoleon: the Last Phase," published in 1900. It would be affectation to ignore the fact that the favourable reception with which this book has been received is due in great measure to the author's eminent name and position. His own modest description of the genesis of the book is such as to disarm hostile criticism: "It was written," says Lord Rosebery, "to lay a literary ghost, dormant for years, only quickened into activity by the analysis of Gourgaud's last journals, and by stimulating leisure."[1] Lord Rosebery gives quite an undue prominence to General Gourgaud, who was after all

[1] "Napoleon: the Last Phase," p. 222.

nothing but a big baby according to the testimony of himself, while he was something rather less harmless according to the testimony of others. Gourgaud is the second hero of Lord Rosebery's book, and his "Journal," we are told, is about the only source of truth at St. Helena! But we shall have more to say of him later. Some critics have accepted this book as a final statement of the St. Helena history, after which nothing need be said. This attitude on their part is all the more remarkable, inasmuch as Lord Rosebery is at no pains to conceal his low opinion of the reader's intelligence. There are several inaccuracies in matters of fact of which not much account need be taken, as few books are free from them; but what is more unusual is that Lord Rosebery does not care to be consistent with himself. Thus Napoleon, according to Lord Rosebery, was a liar, forger, murderer, colossal egotist, etc., and yet further on (p. 247) it is thought worth while to raise the question: "Was Napoleon a good man?" (though "not of course good in the sense that Wilberforce or St. Francis was good"). As we are also informed that ordinary tests and measures of morality do not apply to him, it is difficult to discuss the suggested "goodness"—if the meaning of that word is to undergo some Napoleonic transformation. Again, when Lord Rosebery is hard pressed to explain away the eccentricities of his favourite Gourgaud, "we are rather inclined to believe," he says at one time, "that he is mystifying

Lowe, Bathurst, and Stürmer, to gratify his own sense of humour" and "across an abyss of eighty years we seem to see him wink." At another time this "strange creature" sends Montholon a challenge and, "with his usual unconsciousness of humour, sends with the challenge a gun and six louis which he had borrowed of his enemy."[1] A "strange creature" at the best; but, according to Lord Rosebery, an impossible creature. Again, when Napoleon wished to assume a feigned name, Sir Hudson Lowe fell in with the suggestion and wrote: "If he [Napoleon] wishes to assume a feigned name, why does he not propose one?" Napoleon took him at his word, and so put him "eternally in the wrong," remarks Lord Rosebery. As a fact Sir Hudson Lowe was always willing, thinking it would make matters smoother, and it was Lord Bathurst who objected to Napoleon's assumption of a feigned name. Lord Rosebery is aware of this, and writes on the very next page: "But Napoleon had thus done his best: he could do no more: the blame and responsibility for all further embarrassment about title must remain not with him, not even with Lowe, but with the Ministers of George IV."[2] This is perfectly just, but how then is Lowe put eternally in the wrong? It is unnecessary to give further examples.

Another peculiarity of Lord Rosebery's method is

---

[1] "Napoleon: the Last Phase," pp. 38, 54.
[2] *Ibid.*, pp. 90, 91.

to qualify a statement by the words *it was said* or *it
was alleged*, so that the reader naturally supposes that
the statement is true, or at any rate true in the writer's
opinion. Such a supposition, however, is by no means
justified. In one case Lord Rosebery has informed us
that he did not himself believe the particular statement
to be true, although he made it to score a rhetorical
point, while as regards others one can hardly think
Lord Rosebery believed them, as the least investiga-
tion would have shown their want of truth. He writes,
for instance, of the transhipment of Napoleon and
his suite to the *Northumberland* off Berry Head:
" They were packed like herrings in a barrel. The
Northumberland, it was said, had been arrested on her
way back from India in order to convey Napoleon;
all the water on board, it was alleged, had also been
to India, was discoloured and tainted, as well as short
in quantity." [1]

Now none of these things, though no doubt they
were *said* or *alleged*, were true in fact, and Lord Rosebery is in a position to know they were not true, for
in such a well-known book as Ussher and Glover's
"Napoleon's Last Voyages" we read that the *Northumberland* was in the Medway in July and was fitted out
at Portsmouth (where supplies of fresh water were
usually kept). Captain Ross and Glover gave up their
respective cabins to the Bertrands and Montholons,
while Napoleon expressed himself as well satisfied with

[1] Rosebery, p. 64.

his own accommodation.[1] This can hardly be considered a fair method of writing what purports to be history.

Amid all his inconsistencies and peculiarities, however, Lord Rosebery is consistent in one thing—he is scrupulously unfair to Sir Hudson Lowe. Not a thing can the Governor do, not a word can he say, without becoming the butt of Lord Rosebery's wit and sarcasm. If he makes the mistake of inviting Napoleon to dinner under the title of General Bonaparte (which was the only title Sir Hudson Lowe was empowered to use), it becomes an "amiable condescension" on his part. If he raises the allowance for Napoleon from £8,000 to £12,000 without waiting for orders from England, it is the Governor "magnanimously raising the captive to an equality with himself." If he turns out some rabbits for Napoleon to shoot, "with his unlucky inopportuneness he chooses the moment when the Emperor has been planting some young trees." In order to give colour to the denunciation of Sir Hudson Lowe, the evidence in his favour is systematically depreciated. The great book of offence is of course Forsyth's, which is ridiculed as a "murky compilation" with "gloomy recesses," "a dull and trackless collection," and "a dreary book crowned by a barren index" (why barren? An index is not generally intended to be amusing). In reply to this it is enough to quote the remark of M. de Viel-Castel, who, as a

[1] See "Napoleon's Last Voyages," pp. 91, 99; Rose's "Life of Napoleon I.," ii. 534 n.

Frenchman, would naturally be impatient of want of logical arrangement and want of lucidity. He writes : "J'espère du moins inspirer aux rares amis de la vérité le désir d'aller la chercher à sa source, en bravant la fatigue d'une lecture que la prolixité inévitable d'un mémoire apologetique rend peu attrayante, malgré l'ordre lucide que l'auteur a porté dans la distribution de ses immenses matériaux, malgré la clarté et la simplicité de son style." [1]

But the object of Forsyth was very different from that of Lord Rosebery. The latter is only concerned to " lay a literary ghost," which apparently does not require much trouble ; Forsyth's object was to go carefully through the whole of the correspondence and transactions at St. Helena, to sift the wheat from the chaff, to investigate thoroughly all the charges made against the Governor, and to present an honest account of what took place, based on the most trustworthy evidence obtainable. Truth does not always lend itself to epigrammatic treatment, and the ordinary reader, if not greatly interested in the subject, will find the narrative occasionally tedious and too minute. At the same time the reputation of Forsyth's book is too solidly established to be damaged by Lord Rosebery's popguns, and no serious investigator can do without it, for he will find there a collection of original documents of the first importance for forming a judgement. The two principal first-hand witnesses in favour of

[1] " Revue des Deux Mondes," 1855, vol. ix. p. 293.

Sir Hudson Lowe are the surgeon, Mr. Walter Henry, and Lieut.-Col. Basil Jackson. Their evidence is considered later. Here it need only be said that Lord Rosebery sneers at Henry and absolutely ignores Jackson. It is true that Jackson's "Notes and Reminiscences" was originally printed only for private circulation; still it was not inaccessible to Napoleonic students, and much of the part relating to St. Helena was published in the "United Service Magazine" in 1843. Moreover I gave copious extracts from it in my previous volume, "Sir Hudson Lowe and Napoleon," with which Lord Rosebery shows his acquaintance. Both these gentlemen give strong evidence for the Governor simply as the result of their own observation and experience.

It will be asked why it is that Lord Rosebery has done his best to revive all the original animosity against Sir Hudson Lowe. The answer to this question must, we fear, remain Lord Rosebery's secret; but it may be suggested that Sir Hudson Lowe is guilty of what is in Lord Rosebery's eyes the unpardonable sin—he is entirely without a sense of humour. He was quite unable to appreciate the comic side of his position as the person charged with the custody of Napoleon; he saw only the seriousness and responsibility of it. It may also be suggested that Lord Rosebery heightens the effect and pathos of his eulogy on Napoleon by depicting him as at the mercy of an unsympathetic and tyrannical jailer. Perhaps, after all, Lord

Rosebery's dislike may be merely irrational, and due to the same sort of *enfantillage* which possessed Napoleon—as he admitted himself—at the sight of Lowe. As a work of art the book suffers from the undue prominence given to Gourgaud, but it is lively and agreeable reading for the first time, and most people will read it only once. To read it a second time is not so easy, and the continued epigrams begin to weary. Lord Rosebery does not apparently realize the fact that truth has more than one aspect. The truth of the spoken word is not the same as that of the written word. A casual word thrown out at random in the course of conversation may, if reproduced in writing, impart an entirely false notion—may become, in short, a lie. Lord Rosebery in this book is an "impressionist," as much an impressionist as Froude in his "Life of Carlyle," or Purcell in his "Life of Manning." If a man in a moment of irritation utters a hasty word or writes a hasty letter, it is an act of cruelty and injustice to send it to the printer. "Lady Granville," says Lord Rosebery, "who saw Sir Hudson Lowe two years after he had left St. Helena, said that he had the countenance of a devil."[1] This is hardly worth repeating in any case, but it is rather hard on Lady Granville to embalm it in a book eighty years afterwards. Again, in a conversation with Count Balmain, Sir Hudson Lowe is reported to have said: "Dr. O'Meara has committed unpardonable faults; he informed the

[1] "Napoleon: the Last Phase," p. 66.

people of what goes on in the town, in the country and on board the ships; he went in search of news for them and paid base court to them. Then he gave an Englishman from Bonaparte, and secretly, a snuffbox. What infamy! And is it not disgraceful of this *grandissime* emperor thus to break the regulations?"[1] And Lord Rosebery assures us that this is not burlesque but actually true. But what if it is true? It seems to us very exaggerated, and the notion that Napoleon should be expected to observe the regulations a little absurd; but if it is considered that the Governor was not speaking officially, that he had no reason to suppose that what he said would be repeated, and that Balmain was not in Napoleon's interest, few people will think that it shows anything more than nervousness and over-anxiety that instructions should be followed. What character could stand against such criticism as this? It is as if a man were to be photographed when his features were distorted with anger or his cheek swollen with toothache, and the result were to be exhibited as a permanent likeness.

It has been necessary to write on Lord Rosebery's book at some length because, whatever its demerits, the eminence of the author will always secure for it a certain attention. Already it has been quoted as history. Thus General Ben Viljoen writes of his own captivity at St. Helena: "Our unhappy lot was ren-

[1] Balmain in "Revue Bleue," 1897, vol. vii. p. 680, quoted in Rosebery, p. 72.

dered unnecessarily unpleasant by the insulting treatment offered us by Colonel Price, who appeared to me an excellent prototype [*sic*] of Napoleon's custodian, Sir Hudson Lowe. One has only to read Lord Rosebery's work, 'The Last Phase of Napoleon,' to realize the insults and indignities Sir Hudson Lowe heaped upon a gallant enemy." [1]

Another recent publication dealing with a part of the St. Helena history is "With Napoleon at St. Helena," by M. Paul Frémeaux, which contains a portion of the diary of Mr. John Stokoe, the surgeon of the *Conqueror*. Seeing that Mr. Stokoe was in attendance on Napoleon for one week out of a period of five and a half years, the title is rather pretentious and misleading. While sympathizing with the piety of Miss Stokoe in her desire to vindicate the memory of her great-uncle, we cannot but think that her mode of publication is unwise and her choice of an editor unfortunate. Mr. Stokoe's diary furnishes material for one or two magazine articles, and would have been interesting enough if published by itself. But, as it is, the text of the "diary" is swamped by what Lord Rosebery might call the "murky compilation" of M. Frémeaux. No slur rests on the memory of Stokoe. He was a well-meaning but rather weak man, and, unfortunately for him, his person became for a few

[1] "My Reminiscences," by General Ben Viljoen, 1902. It is evident that General Viljoen (or his translator) is ignorant of the meaning of the word "prototype."

days the centre round which the storm raged at St. Helena. A little cockboat has no chance among iron-clads, and Stokoe naturally suffered. He was sent home, not under arrest, as Mr. Henry states,[1] and then almost immediately sent back to St. Helena under arrest to be tried by court-martial for having violated certain standing orders. He defended himself with eloquence and spirit, but was found guilty and sentenced to be dismissed, though subsequently allowed a pension on account of long and meritorious service. He certainly had hard measure dealt out to him both by the authorities at home and at St. Helena, but there does not appear to be any evidence that the court-martial was terrorized by the Governor and the Admiral as is here represented. Admiral Plampin does not come well out of the affair, but there is nothing that reflects upon Sir Hudson Lowe. M. Frémeaux's contribution—which forms far the larger portion of the book—is not worth criticizing, as his ignorance of the subject is so complete. He is sufficiently inept to place as a motto on the title-page the saying of Napoleon that he would have lived to eighty years if they had not sent him to that island. That Napoleon died of cancer in the stomach, and not of the climate of St. Helena, has been universally accepted by those who regard facts since the *post mortem* examination eighty-two years ago, though the climate theory still forms part of the Napoleonic Legend. M. Frémeaux

[1] "Events of a Military Life," ii. 52.

lets his zeal run away with him when he suggests that there was an " unholy compact " between Sir Hudson Lowe and Admiral Plampin to the effect that, if the Governor would let the Admiral live as he liked (he had in fact been guilty of the folly of bringing a mistress with him), the Admiral would not interfere with the Governor's treatment of Napoleon!

The books above named are all devoted exclusively to St. Helena events. Of general histories which, of course, deal more succinctly with this period, we have the monumental " Life of Napoleon " by Professor W. M. Sloane, Mr. T. E. Watson's " Napoleon I." (both American writers), and the " Life of Napoleon " by Dr. J. Holland Rose. Professor Sloane in his careful work is not unfair to Sir Hudson Lowe when he writes of him: " He was a creature of routine. . . . Neither irascible, severe, nor ill-natured, he was yet punctilious, and in no case a match for the brilliant genius of his antagonist." [1] Lowe was something more than a creature of routine, but he was punctilious without doubt. By nature he was irascible, but as he never showed any temper in the presence of Napoleon it is not of much importance. Admiral Malcolm once defended him by saying that " his temper was too quick to be cunning."

The book of Mr. Watson is on a lower level. It professes to be a popular history of Napoleon, but is in fact a popular account of the Napoleonic Legend.

[1] Vol. iv. p. 216.

It resembles a declamation of some late Greek or Roman sophist in which fact is entirely subordinated to rhetorical effect. His two sources of inspiration are admiration of Napoleon and hatred of this country, and more especially of the Duke of Wellington and (when he comes to St. Helena) of "his tool," [1] Sir Hudson Lowe. He even drags in the Boer War, and quotes as history Montholon's well-invented story of the attempt to make Napoleon surrender his sword— a story which belongs to the Legend. [2] The work of Dr. Holland Rose is of another stamp. It is now widely recognized as the best general history of Napoleon in English. He has taken especial pains with the chapter on St. Helena, and several times has occasion to correct the errors of Lord Rosebery. Sir Hud-

---

[1] How far Sir Hudson Lowe was from being the tool of the Duke of Wellington will appear later.

[2] According to Montholon ("Récits," i. 118), Lord Keith said to him in a voice stifled by emotion: "'England demands your sword.' The Emperor, with a convulsive movement, placed his hand upon the sword that an Englishman dared to demand. The terrible expression of his face was his only answer. Never had it been more powerful, more superhuman. The old Admiral felt himself struck as by lightning; his tall figure shrank away, and his head, white with years, fell on his breast like that of a culprit who humiliates himself before his sentence. The Emperor kept his sword." As a matter of fact Captain Maitland was expressly told by Lord Keith not to make such a request to the fallen Emperor. Unfortunately also this story is contradicted by Las Cases, to whom Lord Keith said that Napoleon's sword would be respected (Las Cases, "Journal," ed. 1824, i. 102). See Forsyth, i. 21 n., and Rose's "Napoleon I.," ii. 528.

son Lowe is here strenuously defended against his detractors.

Of late years some French writers have become less unreasonable. Besides the passages from Lamartine and the review article by M. de Viel-Castel already mentioned, we may refer to the article "Lowe" in Larousse's "Grand Dictionnaire," which contains the following remarkable sentence : "La vérité est que les exigences tyranniques du vaincu rendirent presque impossible au malheureux gouverneur la conciliation des devoirs d'humanité avec les obligations de sa charge et les instructions qu'il avait reçues."

German writers have, on the whole, been much influenced by the Napoleonic Legend. Of recent works we may mention Fournier's "Napoleon I." in the series entitled "Das Wissen des Gegenwart"; Holzhausen's "Napoleon's Tod," written by a worshipper at the temple ; and "Napoleon," edited by Dr. J. von Pflugk-Harttung, of which the St. Helena portion is excellently told by Professor Dr. E. Meyer, of Berlin, who speaks of Sir Hudson Lowe as "obviously one of the most calumniated figures in history."[1]

In days past Sir Hudson Lowe has been, as Forsyth puts it, a *bête noire* of the French imagination ; but Truth, it is said, is the daughter of Time,[2] and I have

---

[1] Vol. ii. Part VI. p. 480. "Lowe ist offenbar eine der schwerstverleumdeten Persönlichkeiten der Geschichte."

[2] "Recte enim Veritas Temporis filia dicitur, non Authoritatis" (Bacon, "Nov. Org. I.," aph. 84).

written the following pages in the hope that the fair-minded Frenchman and the average Englishman may now be disposed to regard the events at St. Helena in the dry light of historical fact. There is, however, another quality of Truth that is not so much observed —it only irritates those whom it fails to convince, and there are some people whose prejudices are so much a part of their nature that the destruction of the former might have the undesirable result of impairing their general mental capacity. To such I make no appeal. I have purposely refrained from discussing the conversations of Napoleon or any part of his history at St. Helena unconnected with the captivity, and, as regards Sir Hudson Lowe, I confine myself as much as possible to his relations with Napoleon, though no doubt his relations to the French attendants and to the British under his rule throw light upon his character, and are therefore not left entirely unnoticed.

CHAPTER II

LOWE'S AUTOBIOGRAPHY

Birth and education.—Gibraltar.—In Italy.—Corsica.—Elba.—
Minorca.—The Corsican Rangers organized.

SIR HUDSON LOWE left behind him a fragment
of an autobiography. This was prepared for
publication more than fifty years ago by Sir Harris
Nicolas—certain portions of no interest being omitted
—and I reproduce it here. Forsyth has published
extracts from it.

"I was born in the Army. My father [1] was an Englishman, a native of Lincolnshire. He was bred to the
study of physic, and obtained a medical appointment
early in life with the troops that served in Germany
during the Seven Years' War. He was present at
the battle of Minden, and at all the principal actions

[1] John Hudson Lowe. "His ancestors had been settled for
several generations in the county of Lincoln, where they farmed
a small property near Grantham, in which town he was born.
He was educated at Stamford, in the same county, and bred to
the study of physic: he took his degree afterwards as Doctor of
Physic at St. Andrews University in Scotland" (From an
introductory draft of a few pages left incomplete by Sir Hudson
Lowe).

27

in which the British troops were engaged during that war. At its close he was appointed to the 50th Regiment, in which corps he served until after the breaking out of the war of the French Revolution, when he was appointed Surgeon-Major and head of the medical department in the garrison of Gibraltar, the duties of which he continued to discharge until his death.[1]

"My mother's maiden name was Morgan, of an ancient and highly respected family in the county of Galway, in Ireland. I was born in the town of that name, on the 28th of July, 1769.[2] My godfathers were General Calcraft, at that time Lieutenant-Colonel of the regiment, and Captain Tisdall.[3] Shortly after my birth the 50th Regiment was ordered to the West Indies, and I was taken out with it. Its first destination was the island of St. Vincent, where I had the misfortune to lose my mother and an only sister, at a period of life which has never since failed to awaken in my mind the most painful recollections. The regiment's next destination was the island of Jamaica, where it remained about three years. The Governor of the island at that time was Sir John Dalling, who was Lieutenant-Colonel of the regiment, and I have

[1] In 1801.

[2] Sir Hudson Lowe was thus a few days older than Napoleon. It is singular that 1769 witnessed the birth also of the Duke of Wellington, Marshals Ney, Lannes, and Soult, and Lord Castlereagh.

[3] An anecdote of this officer occurs in Horace Walpole's Letters.

still a very pleasing recollection of the great kindness
with which I was treated by his family. Upon the
breaking out of the American War the 50th Regiment
was ordered to New York, whither I also accompanied
it, and my earliest recollections of military life date
from that period. I have still in remembrance the
display of military force which was then assembled,
not omitting the whiskered Hessians, whose camp my
father took me to visit, having formed an acquaintance
with some of their officers during the German War.
The regiment was not destined to form part of the
army, but had been ordered to New York to be .
drafted into other corps. After this operation was
over the skeleton of the corps was ordered home. Its
first station was Salisbury, and I was immediately
placed at the grammar-school in that city,[1] at that
time kept by the Rev. Dr. Butt, and afterwards by
Dr. Skinner, where I obtained the first rudiments of
such education as my father's means enabled him to
afford me, chiefly in the classics. During the time of
my being at school, and before I had attained my
twelfth year, I was appointed to an ensigncy in the
East Devon Militia, through the recommendation of
Lord Hinton, then Lord-Lieutenant of the county,
and actually passed a review in my uniform at that
age. I continued to hold my commission until the
signature of the treaty of peace between England and

[1] Sir Hudson Lowe cherished through life a warm attachment
for that city and its beautiful cathedral.

America, when I was recommended by Sir Thomas Spencer Wilson, who at that time commanded the 50th, for the first vacancy that might occur in the corps. An objection was made on account of my youth, when Sir Thomas Wilson was pleased to direct that I should be considered as a volunteer until I had attained the proper age to be appointed to a commission. An opportunity did not occur until the autumn of the year 1787, when I obtained my first King's commission as Ensign in the 50th, on the 25th of September.

"The 50th was at that time stationed at Gibraltar, the Governor being the celebrated Sir George Augustus Elliot, afterwards promoted to the peerage by the title of Lord Heathfield. The works of the fortress were still in the most ruinous state from the effects of the siege. The whole rock was literally covered with fragments of broken shells and shot, and there was not a house in the town, nor a building within the batteries, which did not bear the marks of its devastation.

"Sir George Elliot was succeeded in the command by General O'Hara, who pursued exactly the same course of discipline, with even an additional degree of personal zeal and activity. It was the custom at that time for one of the subalterns of the land-post guard to accompany with an escort the post-sergeant, who proceeded with the keys to open the barrier towards the neutral ground. To those who have served at Gibraltar, the violence with which the easterly winds, or black Levanters as they are called, whirl in eddies round the rock, accompanied by the most terrible gusts of sleet and rain, must be sufficiently known. I was once proceeding with the escort in order to reach the barrier-gate by daybreak, and was moving with my head down, to stem, as well as I was able, the tremendous gusts of rain and wind which opposed me, when I heard myself very sharply spoken to by a mounted officer, who desired me 'to hold up my head, and look what I was about, for it was not as a mere matter of form I was ordered on that duty.' This officer was General O'Hara, who was on such occasions always the foremost to observe that the public duty was rightly performed. This was the *only real rebuke* I ever experienced from a superior officer during the whole course of my military life. I admitted its point as well as its justice, and am proud to believe the beneficial effect was not wholly lost upon me. I might cite instances of praise bestowed upon my conduct by the same distinguished officer, and even of services he afterwards rendered me ; but I relate only the above, because conveying what appears to me a really useful lesson. General O'Hara was not less remarkable than his predecessor for his hospitality, and it was certainly no ordinary gratification to be invited to his table, for there were few men of his day who had so much natural wit, or whose conversation was so sure to enliven any society. It was during the period of his command that the father of her present Majesty, then Prince Edward, came to Gibraltar to be instructed in his profession. He then bore the rank of Colonel,[1] and was appointed to the command of the 2nd or Queen's Regiment, and soon afterwards to that of the 7th or Royal Fusileers, on their being ordered out from England. It is impossible to speak too highly of the correct and practical manner in which his Royal Highness discharged every part of his regimental and general duty. It was not, however, simply a matter of choice with him, for, though he was the last person to need a spur, he was under the command of an officer who would not suffer any species of neglect. Upon one occasion, at a guard-mounting parade, it is in my recollection that some little innovation had been introduced by Prince Edward which did not happen to meet General O'Hara's ideas, and a reproof was conveyed to him in the hearing of the officers assembled. ' I hope, Sir,' said Prince Edward, ' I shall always do my duty.' ' And if you do not do

---

[1] The following extract from a note from the Duke of Kent to Sir Hudson Lowe, recommending an officer to his attention, dated Kensington Palace, 3rd April, 1815, shows his Royal Highness's esteem for Sir Hudson's father: " The Duke, from the knowledge he had of Sir Hudson Lowe's respected father, cannot consider him as a stranger, and therefore has ventured in this instance to treat him with the freedom of an old acquaintance, with which he feels sure that he will not be offended, more especially if he has it in his power to avail himself of Ensign Sedley's services, as the Duke is sure that young man cannot fail of doing credit to his recommendation."

so, Sir, I will make you do it,' was General O'Hara's reply. I mention this as characteristic of the high feeling of both parties—a conscious purity of intention on the part of the late Duke of Kent, and the unawed, though perhaps rudely shown, independent feeling of the gallant and distinguished man under whose guidance he was to receive his first lessons of military subordination as well as military instruction.

" Having been more than four years [1] upon garrison duty, during which time every third or fourth night was passed on guard, with no other appliances for repose, between the reliefs of sentries, than a blanket upon boards and a pillow resting generally upon a stone, I was happy to avail myself of my turn for leave of absence. It afforded me no small gratification to find myself at liberty, as I conceived, for a year and a half, to pass my time in travelling, instead of proceeding direct to England, as was the custom of most officers. I had already made myself sufficiently acquainted with the French, Italian, and Spanish languages to enable me to travel with some degree of comfort in those countries ; but, considering that I might always find an opportunity of visiting Spain while the regiment remained at Gibraltar, I resolved that my first trip should be to France. I had made my arrangements for proceeding to Marseilles when the news of the events which were taking place in that country turned me aside from all intention of then visiting it.

[1] He obtained his lieutenancy on the 11th of November, 1791.

" It was in the month of September, 1792, that this change of plan took place, and, instead of proceeding to Marseilles, I took my passage for Leghorn. It was my first object on arriving in Italy to make myself thoroughly acquainted with the language. I therefore settled myself for nearly three months at Pisa, studying it with such assiduity as to render it afterwards perfectly familiar to me."

At Pisa, Lieutenant Lowe became acquainted with Captain Broome, of the East India Company's service, the author of witty parodies of all the speeches in Westminster Hall on Warren Hastings' trial : [1]

" To the astonishment of the public at the time, he turned them off-hand into crambo rhyme, so that they appeared in the paper at the same time with the report of the speeches as actually delivered. He told me that he never turned over a leaf in writing them, but wrote them off on detached half-sheets of paper. With this gentleman and his family I afterwards travelled to Rome and Naples, and need scarcely add that their society proved not one of the least agreeable recollections of my first peregrination.

" Upon my return to Gibraltar I found the whole garrison in a state of the greatest excitement, in consequence of the breaking out of the war. The animation produced in the garrison was at its height upon

[1] The title of these parodies was "Letters from Simkin the Second to his Brother in Wales."

the arrival of the British fleet in the bay of Gibraltar, under the command of Lord Hood. Soon afterwards the 50th and 51st Regiments, the latter then under the command of Lieutenant-Colonel Moore,[1] were called upon to proceed to Toulon. The *Colossus*, Captain Pole,[2] and the *Fortitude*, Captain Young,[3] came down to take them there. The company which I commanded (for, although only a lieutenant, I had the charge of what was then the Lieutenant-Colonel's company) was embarked on board the *Colossus*. In four days we were off Toulon, when we found that the post had been evacuated,[4] and that the fleet was collected in Hières Bay.

" I had been invited to dine in the cabin on the day we arrived in the bay, and just as we were sitting down to dinner another guest was announced. This was Captain Hood of the *Juno*, afterwards Sir Samuel Hood. He had just then made his escape from the port of Toulon, not knowing that the British fleet had evacuated it, the French having kept the white flag flying, in order to deceive any new-coming vessels. Not suspecting any trick of such a kind, Captain Hood had passed all the first batteries, and was approaching the inner harbour, when a boat came alongside with some French

---

[1] Afterwards the celebrated Lieutenant-General Sir John Moore, K.B.

[2] Afterwards Admiral Sir Charles Morice Pole, Bart., G.C.B.

[3] Afterwards Admiral Sir William Young, G.C.B.

[4] Toulon was evacuated on the 19th of December, 1793.

republican officers on board. They announced to him the change of circumstances, but endeavoured to console him by saying, 'Soyez tranquille, Monsieur, vous serez parfaitement bien traité.' Captain Hood made no answer to them, but turning round to the helmsman said, 'Helm a-lee, about ship, all hands make sail.' In a moment the matter was understood, every man was at his post, the ship was put upon another tack, and in full sail out of the harbour. A rattling fire was soon commenced from the batteries, but did no mischief, and when Captain Hood saw himself out of all danger, he then found leisure to attend to his visitors, and begged them to walk below, saying, 'Soyez tranquilles, Messieurs, vous serez parfaitement bien traités.' [1]

" The whole of the regiment was immediately afterwards removed into the *Fortitude*, and it was soon rumoured that we were all destined to proceed to Corsica. It was necessary for some purpose of fitting out that we should first proceed to Porto Ferrajo, in the island of Elba. Our stay at Porto Ferrajo was short, only time enough to enable us to admire the fortress and general beauty of the island. We proceeded soon after to Corsica, were landed in the outer part of the bay of San Firenze, and immediately proceeded to invest the celebrated martello tower, that which afterwards gave its name to so many expensive,

[1] This anecdote is also told in the accounts of Sir Samuel Hood's life.

injudicious, and unsuitable constructions of the same kind on our own coast."

A long account follows of the operations in Corsica, but only such passages as relate to the writer himself will be inserted. Speaking of the attack on Fort Moselle, he says :

" My duty was principally upon the battery which had been constructed on the night of the assault to the right of the fort. I was a witness of the following circumstances. There were three officers standing upon the battery : they were Lieutenant Anderson, of the 50th ; Lieutenant Byron, of the 15th ; and Ensign Boggis, of the 51st. Their persons stood exposed. Anderson had a sharp eye ; he said to the two others, ' They are pointing at us ; get down.' Anderson himself did so ; the other two disregarding his caution, a shot came from the enemy's battery and killed them both instantly."

The fever with which the troops were attacked is then described; and he says the 50th was ordered to return to Bastia :

" I was embarked with about two hundred men of the 50th Regiment, and a proportionate number of officers, most of whom were of a superior rank to myself. There was no medical officer on board, and I was the only officer who had not been attacked by the fever,

nor were there above twenty men in the vessel who were
not dangerously ill with it. A large supply of bark had
been put on board, and my constant duty was to see
this mixed up in a large camp kettle two or three times
a day, and have it served out to the suffering persons,
in the same manner as upon other occasions I should
have superintended the distribution of their messes.
The 50th Regiment lost above two hundred men by
this fever. Upon our arrival at Bastia it was found
that the regiment was in want of necessary supplies of
every kind, and, as I had been before at Leghorn, I
offered my services to Colonel Wauchope to proceed
there, to procure all that might be wanting both for
officers and men. My offer was immediately accepted,
and I embarked accordingly. The distance was only
sixty miles, but before I got half-way over I found I
was doomed not to escape from the effects of the fever,
for I was suddenly struck down by it with such fierce-
ness that upon my arrival at Leghorn it was with
some difficulty I was enabled to reach the hotel which
was to be my resting place. A good constitution carried
me through, but not until I had been brought to death's
door; so much so, that at one moment I had actually
lost all sense of my existence. I had fortunately formed
acquaintances there on my first visit in the house of
Messrs. Harry and Abel Fonnereau, and they had recommended to me a very able medical man. It so
occurred that, knowing the medical officer attached to
the troops at Corsica had come over in another vessel

at the same time, I sent to ask him to call upon me, when I received a verbal communication that he was attached to the medical staff of the army as a surgeon, and not as a physician. This circumstance, having afterwards reached the ear of Sir Charles Stuart, brought on, as I understood, a fury of indignation against the person who had sent this excuse. The attack of fever was not of long duration, and I was soon enabled to execute the commissions with which I had been charged and to return to Bastia, when I found the destination of the 50th was to form the garrison of Ajaccio. Sir Charles Stuart in the meanwhile had been visiting that quarter.

"We were all delighted with our change of quarters to Ajaccio. The town was well laid out, spacious, well-built, and the citadel had excellent accommodation, but not sufficient for all the officers. One of the best houses in the town was occupied by the mother and sisters of Bonaparte. The present General De Butts, of the Engineers, then a lieutenant in that corps, had been sent forward to provide quarters, and to intimate to the family that, as their sons were in the French service, or had quitted the island, they must surrender their house for the use of the English garrison. An officer of the 50th, of the name of Ford, was for a short time quartered in their house, and spoke with much satisfaction of the kind manner in which the family acted towards him—the young girls, for such they were at that time, running slipshod about the house, but hardly any notice was taken of them. There were several balls and parties given shortly after our arrival there; but Madame Bonaparte was not invited to them, on account of the situation of her sons. She soon after removed to Cargise, which had been originally a Greek colony, to a house which had been built or occupied by Count Marbœuf, whilst at the head of the French administration in that part of the island. It is not from my own recollection I mention these circumstances, because, strange as it may appear, I was not aware of the residence of any part of the Bonaparte family at Ajaccio during nearly two years we were in garrison in that town.

"I used frequently to hear Napoleon Bonaparte spoken of, but not as connected with the exploit which has been generally mentioned as having given the first early celebrity to his name—his share, namely, in the expulsion of the British from Toulon. The person whom I most frequently recollect to have heard speak of him was Signor Campi, who at that time was employed in our commissariat, and who afterwards, I have understood, acted as secretary to Joseph Bonaparte. Signor Campi used to speak to me with admiration of the intrepidity which he showed in shutting himself up in the building called the Seminary, with a body of the National Guards, and bidding defiance to the Royalist troops who were stationed in the citadel, and who thus became besieged there at the commencement of the Revolution. He also spoke of rather an unsuccessful operation which had been afterwards undertaken against the Maddalena Islands; but I heard not a word at that time of Toulon, which has since appeared to me rather extraordinary.

"Colonel Wauchope had been appointed Governor of Ajaccio, and had taken up his residence in the citadel. He invited me to come and reside with him, and to act as his aide-de-camp. I had not long fulfilled the duties of this situation when I found myself suffering from a return of the fever, and my relapses were so frequent that I was recommended to proceed to Italy for a change of air. I again visited Leghorn, and from thence proceeded to Florence and Bologna. At Florence I obtained such excellent medical advice that I was soon restored to health and strength, and even secured by its effects from any future attacks of the disorder. I cannot avoid mentioning the marked and kind attention with which I myself, and two or three other officers who had come to Florence with the same object, were treated there, even in those quarters where imposition on travellers is most generally practised."

Lieutenant Lowe rejoined his regiment at Ajaccio, and on the evacuation of Corsica accompanied it to Porto Ferrajo, in Elba. On the 25th of September, 1795, he was promoted to a company; and was soon after appointed Deputy Judge-Advocate to the troops. From Elba the 50th Regiment proceeded to Lisbon, and arrived there after a tedious voyage of three months.

" The 50th Regiment remained quartered nearly two years in Portugal, never stirring the whole of the time from Fort St. Juliens. The only advantages which I recollect to have derived from this tour of service in Portugal was that of a familiar acquaintance with the language, some knowledge of the disposition of the people, and of the points of defence and resources of the country against a foreign invasion. This knowledge I obtained, in some degree, by making a tour as far as Oporto, and by occasional short excursions in the neighbourhood of Lisbon. My visit to Oporto took place in company with my old and esteemed commander, Colonel Wauchope of the 50th, who, upon Sir Charles Stuart's recommendation, had been appointed one of the Brigadier-Generals of the force under his command. We passed through Torres Vedras, Legria, Pombal, visited the convent of Batalha, the monastery of Alcobaça, Condeixa, Coimbra, and thence proceeded to Oporto.

"We returned to Lisbon along the coast, and very soon after our return the 50th Regiment received an order to proceed to the East Indies. The vessels had actually arrived to take us and the 51st to that remote station; and, to speak of my own individual feelings, I do not ever recollect to have experienced more pain than to see before me such a prospect at a time when such great events were obviously preparing in Europe. A counter order, however, arrived, and the 51st alone were ordered to be embarked. The 50th were ordered to proceed to Minorca. Upon our arrival there we found, to our great regret, that Sir Charles Stuart, having accomplished the object of his mission, had returned to England ; and we were the more sorry that it was on account of his health."

For Sir Charles Stuart he entertained the most ardent admiration, and he fortunately succeeded in impressing that distinguished officer with a very favourable opinion of his merits. Speaking of Captain Lowe in a letter in December, 1799, Sir Charles, besides other eulogistic expressions, said : "I am glad you have found Captain Lowe useful. I know him to be a young man of honour, information, and merit."

"The command of the island soon afterwards devolved on General Fox, brother of Mr. Fox

"The possession of Minorca paved the way for those operations which were afterwards so successful in obtaining a hold on Malta. The two regiments with which Sir Charles Stuart secured the citadel of Messina were afterwards employed at the blockade of the last-named island. All these services were afterwards forgotten, not on account of any want of intrinsic merit, but solely because the Government of the country did not directly profit by them. No sooner had Sir Charles

Stuart obtained possession of Minorca than a host of emigrants flocked to the island from Corsica, and he speedily organized a small corps of them, to which he gave the title of the *Corsican Rangers*. With this corps my fate and fortunes became afterwards intimately connected."

Here ends the autobiography. " It is to be regretted," adds Sir Harris Nicolas, " that Sir Hudson Lowe did not continue to be his own biographer. Autobiography, however partial, is nevertheless perhaps the most charming of all compositions, and any other account of an eventful life is comparatively cold and inanimate." The materials next in interest to original memoirs are letters ; but, though Sir Hudson Lowe's correspondence after the year 1800 was copious, the space to which this small work must be restricted prevents his letters from being inserted to any extent.

CHAPTER III

THE CORSICAN RANGERS

In Egypt with Moore.—Mission to Portugal.—Capri.—Ischia
and Procida.—Ionian Islands.

THE substance of this chapter will be found in
more detail in Forsyth's third chapter, which is
a memoir of Sir Hudson Lowe. I have, however, given
some particulars from the materials collected by Sir
Harris Nicolas which Forsyth does not give, and from
papers lent by Miss Lowe.

The charge of the newly raised corps of Corsicans
was entrusted to Captain Lowe. In August, 1800, this
corps, then about 200 strong, was sent to Gibraltar to
join the expedition to Egypt under Sir Ralph Aber-
cromby. It formed part of the reserve commanded by
Major-General (afterwards) Sir John Moore. Captain
Lowe held the temporary rank of major. "The vigilance and method with which he conducted outpost
duty," says the writer of the memoir of Sir Hudson
Lowe in the "United Service Magazine,"[1] "was conspicuous, and procured a pointed eulogium from General

[1] April, 1844, p. 593.

Moore. 'Lowe,' were his words, 'when you're at the outposts I always feel sure of a good night's rest.'" Of the Corsican corps and its commander, Sir Robert Wilson writes as follows in his "History of the British Expedition to Egypt": "This corps in every action, and especially in the landing, distinguished itself particularly, and Major Lowe, who commanded it, gained always the highest approbation. Indeed, it was a corps which from its conduct and appearance excited general admiration, and did honour to the nation of the First Consul of France."

After the peace of Amiens Major Lowe was appointed to the 7th Fusiliers, and shortly afterwards one of the permanent Assistant Quartermasters-General. Major-General Moore remained his firm friend, and as it is rightly considered a distinction *laudari a laudato viro*, to be praised by one whom others praise, one of several letters to Major Lowe may be quoted here:

"Chatham, 21st April, 1802.

"MY DEAR LOWE,

"I congratulate you most sincerely on your appointment to the Fusiliers. It is nothing more than you well deserve; and if I have been at all instrumental in bringing it about I shall think the better of myself for it. I hope before we leave that the Fusiliers will be at home, and in a way to be actively employed. I trust you will always consider me as a person warmly interested in your welfare, and that you will

let me hear from you occasionally ; and if duty or
pleasure bring you near me, now or hereafter, you may
depend upon the best reception I can give. Believe
me, very sincerely and faithfully,

"JOHN MOORE."

When the peace proved to be hollow, Major Lowe
was appointed by the Government, in July, 1803, to
proceed on a secret mission to Portugal in order to
inspect the troops and fortresses along the frontier,
and report on the practicability of defending the
country by united British and Portuguese forces. On
the termination of this mission he was employed to
raise the regiment of Royal Corsican Rangers, of which
he was appointed Lieut.-Col. Commandant, and, taking
part in the expedition to Naples under Sir James
Craig, made frequent journeys to Naples and Sicily.
In June, 1806, Lowe was placed by Sir John Stuart
(who had succeeded Sir James Craig) in command of
the island of Capri, which had lately been captured by
Sir Sidney Smith. Here he remained with five companies of the Corsican Rangers as a garrison, which
was subsequently strengthened by the remainder of
the Corsicans and the Maltese Regiment. Soon after
his arrival at Capri, Colonel Lowe showed his humanity by addressing a letter of remonstrance to
General Berthier, then Chief of the Staff of the French
army in Naples, in which he appealed to him to put a
stop to the numerous military executions in Calabria.

While thus employed Sir Hudson Lowe was almost the sole channel of communication through which either the Commander-in-chief in the Mediterranean or the Commanders of the Fleet, or the Foreign Ministers residing in the islands of Sardinia and Sicily, received any correct information respecting the movements and operations of the enemy's armies on the Continent or in Italy. As an instance of the importance of the intelligence he was thus at times able to convey, we may cite the information which he gave to Lord Collingwood of a movement of the French fleet from Toulon. This, not being believed at the time, was not acted on, but its accuracy was afterwards fully acknowledged by Lord Collingwood, who at the same time requested a continuance of Sir Hudson Lowe's communications. He was, too, almost the only channel through which the people of Italy received information of any event adverse to the views and interests of the then ruler of France, as by means of a printing press established on the island of Capri he was able to have all reports of the Spanish victories and of British successes in any quarter affixed in the most public places of the city of Naples, and disseminated throughout Italy within the shortest possible time. We get a glimpse of Colonel Lowe at Capri in the memoir of Sir John Cope Sherbrooke, contained in Mr. Patchett Martin's "Life of Lord Sherbrooke."[1] Sir John was then in Sicily, and corresponded with Colonel Lowe.

[1] Vol. ii. p. 548.

On January 1st, 1808, we find him writing to Lowe for foreign gazettes.

For more than two years Lieutenant-Colonel Lowe was Governor at Capri, until, in October, 1808, the island was attacked by a powerful French naval and military expedition from Naples, then ruled by Murat, and, after a siege of thirteen days, compelled to surrender, chiefly owing to the misconduct of the Maltese regiment and the want of naval assistance. Colonel Lowe, however, refused to come to any other terms than those of a free evacuation with arms and baggage —terms which were after some difficulty accorded. It is true that Sir William Napier, in his "History of the Peninsular War," says that it was at Capri "Sir Hudson Lowe first became known to history, by losing in a few days a post that, without any pretensions to ability, might have been defended for as many years." We cannot be surprised that the enemies of Sir Hudson Lowe have eagerly seized on this unfortunate remark of the illustrious historian, for unfortunate and unjust it is, and it is a sufficient reply to say that officers at the time and near the spot, who had every opportunity of judging, expressed a very different opinion. Thus, Major-General Lord Forbes wrote to Colonel Lowe: "I am convinced that Sir John Stuart will take an early opportunity of expressing to you, as well as to the public, the sense he entertains of the unremitting zeal, ability, and judgement which your conduct has displayed under your late trying circumstances at Capri." And Sir John Stuart himself, the Commander-in-chief, wrote :

"However I am to regret the circumstances of our being dispossessed of a position so strong, and in many respects so useful, as that which we held in the Bay of Naples, yet I am happy to express my perfect satisfaction at your own able, gallant, and judicious conduct, as well as at the zealous and animated support which you acknowledge to have received from your officers and those brave soldiers who adhered to and returned with you hither in the defence of the town of Capri : a point which, after your first most unexpected and unaccountable disaster at Ana Capri, could scarcely any longer be regarded as a military post The honourable terms of convention which you finally obtained test the firmness of your resistance, and as such I venture to hope will be most graciously considered by his Majesty and his Royal Highness the Commander-in-chief; and the article which you established for the security of the inhabitants of the island has been extremely satisfactory to the feelings and solicitude of this Court." [1]

It has also been represented that the garrison consisted of 2,000 men and the French assailants of 1,200; the fact was that the garrison, exclusive of officers,

[1] The Neapolitan Court.

was 1,362 men, while the French were between 3,000 and 4,000.[1] After his return to Sicily, Colonel Lowe felt much annoyance that his official report of the fall of Capri was not published in the " London Gazette," and actually applied for leave to go to England to vindicate his military reputation, and even thought of abandoning his profession. He was, however, dissuaded from leaving by the Commander-in-chief, as the Corsican Rangers were about to form part of an expedition to the Bay of Naples. No doubt the non-publication of his own account gave a handle to his enemies in after years ; but he was somewhat consoled at the time by a very friendly letter from Major-General Oakes,[2] then at Malta, who wrote :

" Indeed, my dear Lowe, I think you feel the thing too keenly when you talk of any treatment from any individual whatever compelling you to quit a profession in which you bear so high a character, have acquired so much honour, and have so many friends. It sometimes happens that political matters, unconnected with military operations, make it necessary to suppress the

[1] On this point Lord Rosebery says (p. 67), referring to Sir Hudson Lowe : " Nor was it any advantage to him to have been driven from Capri by General Lamarque, with, it was alleged, an inferior force." Lord Rosebery here uses against Sir H. Lowe an alleged statement which he ought to know to be contrary to fact.

[2] Afterwards Lieutenant-General Sir Hildebrand Oakes, Bart., G.C.B.

details of services however meritorious in themselves, though they are not the less valued where it is most desirable they should be so, and I suppose this may be the cause why the accounts of the capture of Capri have never been published. This certainly bears hard and is very cruel upon you, because it may serve to impress the minds of some that there have been faults in conducting the defence; and these may for a time, by those who are unacquainted with your talents and character, be attributed to you who commanded."

In June, 1809, under the chief command of Sir John Stuart, Colonel Lowe with his Corsicans formed part of the force that captured the islands of Ischia and Procida, and Lowe made the capitulation of Ischia with the French general, by which the garrison was forced to surrender as prisoners of war. The Corsican Rangers then returned to Sicily, and in September formed part of an expedition to the Ionian Isles under Brigadier-General Oswald. Lieut.-Colonel Lowe was second in command, and conducted the landing on Zante, after which Cephalonia and Cerigo surrendered. General Oswald appointed Lowe to be Governor in Cephalonia, "certain that so delicate a trust could not be reposed in more able hands."[1] He continued to administer the civil government of Cephalonia, with which Ithaca was soon afterwards united, during the end of 1809 and the beginning of 1810. Colonel Lowe

[1] Despatch, October 5th, 1809.

then urged on General Oswald the advisability of securing the island of Santa Maura, which contained a strong fortress and was in immediate proximity to the coast. The expedition was successfully carried out, and Colonel Lowe was thanked three times in the public despatches. The island of Santa Maura was then added to the civil government of Cephalonia and Ithaca, and for nearly two years Colonel Lowe administered it without special remuneration. On his leaving the islands in 1811 General Oswald issued a circular letter, in which he said he was confident "that it would be most grateful to the Government and population of Cephalonia and Ithaca to know that they would still enjoy the benefits arising from the civil administration of an officer who had shown himself the common father of all ranks and classes of their communities."

He prepared a report on the island for the Colonial Office, and on his departure was presented by the grateful inhabitants with an address of thanks and a gold sabre Lowe returned home in February, 1812, on leave, having lately obtained the rank of full colonel. He says: " I was then in my twenty-fourth year of service, and had never been absent a single day from my public duty since the commencement of the war in 1793. I had been in England only once during that time, and then only for a period of six months during the peace of Amiens "

CHAPTER IV

LOWE WITH FOREIGN ARMIES

Stockholm.—Inspection in Russia and Poland.—With the Allies at Bautzen and Leipsic.—With Blücher's army to Paris.—Quartermaster-General in the Low Countries.—Command in South of France.—Appointment to St. Helena.—Reputation of Sir Hudson Lowe at this time.

WHILE Colonel Lowe was making arrangements to return to the Ionian Islands, and within two days of departure, his destination was suddenly changed, and he became a participator in the most wonderful military events that Europe had ever witnessed. He was already known to Government as an active, vigilant, and trustworthy officer, especially fitted for foreign missions on account of his knowledge of languages, when, at the beginning of 1813, he was appointed to a position in which his talents could be displayed on a larger scale. In January he was sent on a secret mission to the north of Europe to inspect the Russian-German legion, a body raised principally from the deserters and prisoners of the contingents impressed by Napoleon into his Russian campaign. Lowe went first to Sweden with Lieut.-General Sir

Alexander Hope and saw Bernadotte, then Prince
Royal, at Stockholm, under whom it was at first intended that the Russian-German Legion should be
placed. In a letter written on the 15th of February,
after informing Colonel Bunbury (then Under-Secretary of State in the War Department) of his arrival,
he thus described his interviews with the King and
Queen and the Crown Prince of Sweden:

"Two days after I had the honour of being introduced, in company with General Hope and his aide-
de-camp, to the King and Prince Royal (Bernadotte).
The former said but little. He merely observed to
General Hope that he hoped matters would be arranged to his satisfaction. The Prince Royal received
us in his own apartment, which we entered through
half-closed doors; his reception of us was perfectly
polite, unreserved, and friendly. His conversation was
entirely with General Hope. After some questions to
the General as to the situation of our armies in Spain,
asking in particular whether it was true that Lord
Wellington had withdrawn any part of his force as far
as Coimbra, and what was the strength of the division
destined to act on the side of Catalonia, we took our
leave. The same day we were invited to dine with
him. He ate much and spoke little. After dinner, and
during coffee, I had the honour of being addressed by
him. He asked me of what corps I wore the uniform,
what was its force, and where stationed; and after en-

quiring as to the time of my departure from hence, which I informed him depended on the communications that might be had with his Royal Highness, he said that he was happy to see me. On the following day we were introduced to the Queen. Count de Neipperg, the Austrian Minister, who had just arrived, was presented at the same time."

On the 19th, Colonel Lowe had a private interview with the Crown Prince and dined with him on the following day. At Stockholm Colonel Lowe met Madame de Staël, of whom and of Bernadotte he sent an interesting description to Colonel Bunbury, which is quoted by Forsyth.[1]

From Stockholm he crossed the Gulf of Bothnia on the ice, and joined Lord Cathcart, the British Ambassador to Russia, at the Emperor Alexander's headquarters at Kalisch in Poland, where he quite won the confidence of that monarch. Colonel Lowe was honoured with a private audience of the Emperor, which he describes in a letter to Colonel Bunbury, and ever after cherished a warm admiration for him.

"To hear from his own mouth," says Lowe, "that he hoped the English people would be satisfied with what he had done, conveyed to me in my own language, with a countenance which beamed with openness, sincerity, and inward satisfaction that he had

[1] Forsyth, i. 104.

followed that course which ought to obtain for him
the goodwill of the people whose esteem was, I firmly
believe, one of the strongest incentives to his line of
action, was highly gratifying, and inspired me with a
respect and consideration towards him, and, if I may
presume to use the expression, attachment, which
every subsequent circumstance the more strengthened
and confirmed."

Colonel Lowe found the corps of which he was in
pursuit—of 2,000 to 3,000 men—scattered over the
country between Narva and Königsberg, a distance of
over 500 miles, and, after performing the duties of
inspection, joined the headquarters of the Allies in
May and was present at the battle of Bautzen, the
20th and 21st of May, on which occasion he had his
first view of Napoleon.   In July, Lowe was ordered
by Lieut.-General Sir Charles Stewart [1] to inspect
the whole of the Hanoverian and German forces in
British pay, amounting to 20,000 men, and was sent
in October to join the Russian and Prussian army
under General Blücher, which he did just before the
battle of Möckern, on the 16th of October. He was
also present at the battle of Leipsic, of which he wrote
a long and interesting account. Colonel Lowe remained with Blücher's army till the beginning of
November, when he returned to his duties in the north

[1] At this time British Minister to Prussia, afterwards third
Marquis of Londonderry.

of Germany. Soon after his temporary removal from
the Prussian army, Colonel Lowe received a letter
from General Count Gneisenau, the Chief of Blücher's
Staff, an officer whose admirable talents are too well
known to need any encomium, in which the following
passage occurs : [1]

" It is with much regret that I have learnt that you
have quitted our headquarters. Your honourable behaviour and good conduct have gained all our hearts.
You have shared our hopes and our fears, and you
have enjoyed with us our victory and triumph. Such
events ought to link together for ever those who serve
with an entire devotion the same cause. Be assured,
then, of our esteem and our attachment, and especially
of my own."

On Blucher's army crossing the Rhine, in January,
1814, Colonel Lowe was ordered by Sir Charles Stewart
to rejoin it, which he did at Vaucouleurs, and from that
moment remained with the Prussian army until the
capture of Paris. He was thus present at thirteen
general engagements (including those of the preceding
year), in eleven of which the enemy's army was com-

[1] Quoted in Forsyth, i. 107. Alison in his " History of Europe,
1789-1815" (xii. 44), says. "What is very remarkable, in com-
bating the modern Hannibal, the Marcellus of the Allies was found
under the grey locks of the Prussian veteran, and the Fabius
in the more youthful breast of his gifted lieutenant."

manded by Napoleon in person. As the only English officer of rank with the Prussian forces Colonel Lowe's position was one of much influence and responsibility. His reports to Sir Charles Stewart, which are remarkable for perspicacity and military ability, were considered so important that upwards of twenty of them were immediately published in the "London Gazette." Some of these documents and the letters from General Count Gneisenau show the manner in which his suggestions were received, and his conduct and opinions considered, at the headquarters of the Prussian army, where he had frequently to oppose the contending arguments of the Austrian and other officers. The unmerited hatred which exists in France against Sir Hudson Lowe will not be lessened when it is known that it was mainly owing to his advice, earnestly and repeatedly urged, that the Prussians marched upon Paris.[1]

To no one in the allied army could the occupation of Paris have been more gratifying than to Colonel Lowe, for to him it was the accomplishment of a plan which he had been the first to conceive and the most

[1] Sir Charles Stewart writes to him from Troyes (February 13th): "I have received with much satisfaction your several reports up to the 12th from your bivouac at La Bergère. My brother [Lord Castlereagh] is much pleased with the clear and detailed manner in which you have kept us informed. I think you are rather too hot for Paris, since we have seen so little spirit among the people; we must not to gain 225 guineas give up gaining 200."

persistent to advocate. His reward was striking and appropriate. It was he who brought the news of Napoleon's abdication to England. He volunteered for this mission, which, from the state of France at that moment, was one of no ordinary danger. Lord Cathcart wrote to him to express a hope that he would not undertake it. He travelled alone with a Cossack orderly, but met with no opposition. The French people had been so decimated by the long war that only old men and boys were in the fields.[1] Arriving at Calais he had no difficulty in procuring a fishing-vessel to carry him across, but the Dover boatmen asked a large sum for landing him.[2] When the news was heard he was warmly welcomed and driven at full speed to London. He arrived on the 9th April and went first to the Foreign Office, whence he was sent on to Carlton House. The Prince Regent was not then dressed, but received him in his bedroom, asked him to dine the same evening, and then conferred on him the honour of knighthood. At dinner Sir Hudson sat between the Prince and Lord Erskine, who were

[1] Sir Harry Smith says in his "Autobiography": "All women in France of moderate or certain age were widows at this period" (i. 189), an intentional exaggeration, of course, but hardly more than an exaggeration.

[2] The passport with which he travelled from Paris was headed "De par l'Empereur et Roi," but signed by the Russian Commandant of Paris. It is now in the British Museum, as is also the passport issued by Sir Hudson Lowe in his own name, with which he travelled from Marseilles to Paris in the following year.

anxious to obtain many details from him, but he was so worn out with fatigue that he could scarcely keep awake. The Prussian Order of Military Merit followed him home, and on his return to Paris the Emperor Alexander conferred on him the Russian Order of St. George. He was promoted in June to the rank of Major-General. During the summer General Lowe was appointed Quartermaster-General of the army in the Netherlands, commanded by the Prince of Orange, and was required to inspect and report on the state of the fortresses to be established as a barrier against France. Among other plans which he proposed for the consideration of the Secretary of State for the War Department and of the Duke of Wellington, he suggested the construction of a work at *Mont St. Jean* (close to Waterloo), it being, in his opinion, the point at which, if the country were invaded, the enemy must be met.[1]

Colonel Basil Jackson—afterwards an intimate friend of Sir Hudson Lowe and at this time a very young

[1] In the "Queries submitted regarding the measures to be taken for the defence of the Belgic provinces, on the supposition of the French Government having any hostile designs against them," the seventh and last query was as follows: "Should any intermediate post be taken up between the frontiers and Brussels, supposing the latter line of operation be thought the most suitable, *query* in respect to the construction of a work at Mont Jean, being the commanding point at the junction of the two principal *chaussées* leading direct from the French frontier on the side of Charleroi and Namur to Brussels, and the line of direction in which an enemy must then move?"

officer on the Staff—thus speaks of his first acquaintance with him :

"About this time Sir Hudson Lowe was appointed
Quartermaster-General, succeeding Colonel, afterwards Lord, Cathcart.[1] . . . His successor proved to
be all we could desire, as an active, diligent, and accomplished officer, who not only worked hard himself
but also kept his officers on the alert, evincing towards
them at the same time the utmost consideration."[2]

In September, Sir Hudson Lowe had occasion to
write to General Count Gneisenau, who in his reply
begins with the following strong expressions of regard
—the original is in French:

"It is with the greatest satisfaction, my very dear
and honoured General, that I have received your letter
of the 15th of September, which tells me that you
have still preserved the remembrance of a man who
is infinitely attached to you, and who in the course of
a memorable campaign, if there ever were one, has
learnt to appreciate your rare military talents, your
profound judgement on the great operations of war,
and your imperturbable *sang-froid* in the day of
battle. These rare qualities and your honourable character will link me to you eternally."

[1] Son of Lord Cathcart, our Ambassador to Russia, mentioned
before.

[2] "Waterloo and St. Helena," p. 4.

Again, to anticipate a little, I am tempted to quote a passage from a letter by the same writer to Sir Hudson at St. Helena, in October, 1817, which well expresses the general confidence felt on the Continent in the vigilance of the Governor—the translation is again from the French :

"Thousands of times have I carried my thoughts over that vast ocean solitude to that interesting rock on which you are the guardian of the public repose of Europe. On your vigilance and on your force of character depends our safety ; if you were to relax your rigorous care against the wiliest villain in the world,[1] if you were to allow your subordinates to grant him any favours through a mistaken pity, our repose would be compromised, and honest folk in Europe would be a prey to their old anxiety. I have often been questioned on this point—I who was known to have the honour of your acquaintance—and I always replied that I could guarantee your loyalty, your sagacity, and your vigilance. The most devoted of your friends, I am so deeply interested in your well-being that I beg you across the sea to have the goodness to give me news of your health, your pleasures, your pains, your domestic happiness, in short of all that can interest a friend."

As we shall see, however, Sir Hudson Lowe showed, in fact, much more leniency to Napoleon than Count

[1] "Le plus rusé scélérat du monde."

Gneisenau would have approved. Field - Marshal Blücher also wrote to Sir Hudson Lowe, in January, 1815, as follows :

"The recollection of a man whom, during so very memorable an epoch as the last campaign, we have learnt to esteem and respect, remains dear to us, and will be ever dearly valued through life. On such grounds you may rely with confidence on the continuance of my attachment and friendship. I wish you joy from my heart on the important post which the Prince Regent, in his confidence, has bestowed upon you, and I rejoice that the choice has fallen upon a man so perfectly equal to fulfil the duties of it in its whole extent."

Sir Hudson Lowe was still Quartermaster-General in the Netherlands when Napoleon landed from Elba in March, 1815, the Prince of Orange being then, as before, Commander-in-chief. The position of Sir Hudson Lowe was now one of the highest importance, and he soon had an opportunity of rendering a signal service to his country, and indeed to Europe. By the authority of the Prince of Orange, he had despatched a letter to the Prussian headquarters urging that their army should be assembled on the Meuse, in a situation where it would be ready to co-operate with the British in the defence of Belgium. Accordingly, in spite of the opposition of General Müffling, General

Kleist and others, who thought Napoleon would move in the direction of Switzerland, the Prussian army proceeded to carry out this suggestion. But now, for political reasons,[1] the Prince of Orange and his father, the King of Holland, drew back, and were desirous of keeping the Prussian army behind the Meuse.

"The Prince of Orange directed me," says Sir Hudson Lowe, in a letter written from St. Helena to Lord Bathurst, "to write to General Kleist or General Müffling accordingly. I told the Prince that, having been the means of making these arrangements with the Prussian army, by which it was approaching to act in concert with the British, I did not feel I could with propriety now write to propose a different plan of operation. The Prince, however, insisted upon the necessity of my writing, saying that the instructions he had received from the King were positive. I then used every argument in my power to convince the Prince, that, as a *military measure*, it was the only one by which the Low Countries could then be saved, that to propose anything contrary would be entirely against my own opinion as the Quartermaster-General of the Army; and finding he still persevered in desiring me to write, I was compelled at last to say to him that I could not consider the determination which had been

---

[1] Montholon afterwards said, at St. Helena, that Napoleon had proposed to the King of Holland that he should give up his claim to Belgium, offering to procure him compensation in the north of Germany.

taken as founded in any reasons of a *military nature*, and that if they were the result of *political considerations* they were not of my competence to write upon; I therefore begged that he would allow me to decline being the medium of communication."

It is perhaps not too much to say that the firmness of Sir Hudson Lowe on this occasion enabled part of the Prussian army to be present at Waterloo. It is pleasing to record that subsequently the Prince of Orange admitted the correctness of Sir Hudson Lowe's judgement, and some twenty years later, when King of Holland, greeted him most warmly at a levée of William IV.

In April the Duke of Wellington arrived to take command of the allied army, and Sir Hudson found himself for the first time in personal relations with the great chief. But this only lasted for a few weeks, for early in May he was offered the command of the British troops in Genoa who were to act with the Austro-Sardinian army and the squadron under Lord Exmouth in the south of France. The offer was too good to be declined, but Sir Hudson, not wishing to leave without the Duke's approbation, waited upon him and communicated the result of the interview in a letter to Sir Henry Bunbury,[1] in which the following passage occurs:

[1] Colonel Bunbury, who became a Major-General in June, 1814, and was made a K.C.B. in January, 1815, was at this time

" He [the Duke] observed that Colonel Sir William
De Lancy might be expected to arrive here in a day
or two, but that he knew not how soon he might be
rendered *au fait* of the duties of the department ;
that Sir George Murray had been with him for six
years, and that he was accustomed to him, but that
he did a good deal of his own business and could do
business with anyone. He said it was a case in which
I must judge for myself. I told him I should be proud
to find I could be of any service to him, and therefore
matters might remain as they were until Sir William
De Lancy's arrival ; that I would write to acquaint
you—which he approved. He remarked that Lord
Bathurst might have particular views in selecting me
for the situation, and I was happy to hear this observation, as it diminished the delicacy I might otherwise
feel in quitting him, and the manner in which he has
borne with my insufficiency makes me naturally desirous not to fail him on this point. In other respects
I have no hesitation about the choice of situation, and
shall address the Duke upon it when Sir William De
Lancy arrives." [1]

Under-Secretary of State in the War Department, and so
remained till 1816.

[1] I quote this letter because it is a decisive answer to the
version of the relations between the Duke of Wellington and
Sir Hudson Lowe given in the notice of the latter in the
"American Cyclopaedia" (vol. x. p. 690). We there read : " He
held this post [of Quartermaster-General] when Napoleon landed
from Elba, but the Duke of Wellington then appointed in his place

The result was that Sir Hudson remained with
the Duke till the beginning of June. The gallant
Sir William Howe De Lancy, who succeeded him
as Quartermaster-General, was struck by a cannon-
ball at Waterloo and died a few days later.[1] Sir
Hudson Lowe soon afterwards married Sir William
De Lancy's sister, the widow of Lieutenant-Colonel
William Johnson. The duties of the British forces in
the south of France turned out to be very light. Marseilles was at once occupied without opposition, and
Toulon yielded to the Royalists on Sir Hudson's approach. The conduct of Sir Hudson Lowe procured
for him the warm esteem of the distinguished Admiral
with whom he had co-operated. "You have, my dear
Sir Hudson," writes Lord Exmouth under the date of
August 27th, 1815, from Marseilles, "my entire esteem

Col. Sir W. De Lancy. . . . He felt acutely the course of the
Duke of Wellington towards him ; and it was owing to this fact,
and as a means of soothing his feelings, that upon the surrender
of Napoleon and his banishment to St. Helena, he was selected
as the Governor of that island and entrusted with the charge of
the great captive." The resentment of Lowe and the means of
soothing his feelings are equally imaginary. Mr. T. E. Watson
goes to the other extreme in calling Sir H. Lowe the "tool" of
the Duke of Wellington at St. Helena. See Appendix A.

[1] Of him the Duke of Wellington wrote in his Waterloo despatch : "I had every reason to be satisfied with the conduct of
the Adjutant-General, Major-General Barnes, who was wounded,
and of the Quartermaster-General, Colonel De Lancy, who was
killed by a cannon-shot in the middle of the action. This
officer is a serious loss to his Majesty's service and to me at
this moment " ("Wellington Despatches," xii. 483).

and regard, and I am sensible, had opportunity been afforded us for more brilliant services, that we should have woven our confidence into the most perfect and lasting friendship." The letter ends with these words : "God bless you, Sir Hudson ; may health, success, and happiness attend you ! Believe me ever, your sincerely and faithfully attached friend, Exmouth." The Municipal Council of Marseilles, it may be mentioned, testified their respect for his conduct during the occupation by voting to him, as well as to Lord Exmouth, a handsome piece of silver plate.

On August 1st, while at Marseilles, Sir Hudson Lowe received a notification that he was appointed to have the charge of the person of Napoleon, who had about a fortnight previously surrendered himself on board the *Bellerophon.* He was directed to return to London immediately, and soon afterwards the East India Company appointed him Governor of St. Helena. The local rank of Lieutenant-General with the command of the troops was conferred upon him, and his salary was fixed at £12,000 per annum. In Paris he had interviews with the Duke of Wellington and Lord Castlereagh. On his arrival in England he received an assurance in Lord Liverpool's name that if he undertook the charge of Napoleon's person, and continued in that charge for three years, "it should not stop there." The rest of his time was occupied in seeing various officials, and in preparations for his voyage. On the last day of the year he was married. On the

23rd of January he was made a K.C.B., and on the 29th started for St. Helena with his family (his wife and two stepdaughters) and suite by the *Phaeton* frigate, which reached the island on April 14th, 1816.

I have been somewhat minute in tracing the earlier career of Sir Hudson Lowe, because, in view of what followed, it is important to keep in mind the public services he had rendered and the reputation which he bore up to this time. In his "Life of Napoleon," Lockhart says of Sir Hudson Lowe that the utmost that could be said against him was that his "antecedents were not splendid." This is not putting the matter fairly. One usually confines the word "splendid" to services which are in themselves exceptionally conspicuous. In this sense the services of Sir Hudson Lowe were not "splendid," nor could they have been so from the nature of the case; but they may be described as most valuable and distinguished services and such as had repeatedly earned the commendation of Government. Many other letters from officers whose merit is well known could have been quoted, all testifying to the high esteem felt for Sir Hudson Lowe; but those already given are perhaps sufficient for the purpose.

It is more to the point to observe that, although it has often been said that Sir Hudson Lowe was not an officer of sufficiently high rank or distinguished career to be entrusted with the custody of Napoleon, this was by no means the opinion of Napoleon himself until he had quarrelled with the Governor. In a well-known letter to Sir Hudson Lowe, dated December 19th, 1816, Count Las Cases writes as follows—and on this particular point it suited him at the moment to speak the truth:

"'A man is appointed to take the command here,' we said (you, sir, were the person alluded to),'who holds a distinguished rank in the army ; he owes his fortune to his personal merit; his life has been passed in diplomatic missions at the headquarters of the Sovereigns of the Continent, where the name, the rank, the power, the titles of the Emperor Napoleon must have become familiar to him.' . . . 'This man,' we said, 'in his diplomatic career will have formed just notions both with respect to persons and things. His arrival alone is therefore a sufficient pledge of the favourable nature of his instructions with respect to us.' '*Did you not tell me,*' said the Emperor to us one day, '*that he was at Champaubert and at Montmirail? We have then probably exchanged a few cannon-balls together, and that is always, in my eyes, a noble relation to stand in.*' Such was the disposition in which Sir Hudson Lowe was expected."

No doubt it is here the object of Las Cases to contrast the expectations they had formed of Sir Hudson Lowe with the reality which (according to their view) they experienced, but these words are con-

clusive testimony to the *nature* of those expectations.
Again, Napoleon said to Colonel Sir George Bingham,
who commanded the troops at St. Helena, when he
heard of the arrival of Sir Hudson Lowe : " I am glad
of it ; I am tired of the Admiral [Sir George Cock-
burn],[1] and there are many points I should like to talk
over with Sir Hudson Lowe. He is a soldier and has
served ; he was with Blücher ; besides, he commanded
the Corsican regiment and knows many of my friends
and acquaintances."[2] Let us then hear no more of
this ; if Napoleon was satisfied with the antecedents
of Sir Hudson Lowe, surely no one else has a right to
complain of them.

The character borne by Sir Hudson Lowe up to
this date may be fairly summed up in the words of
Colonel Basil Jackson, who wrote a short "tribute to
his memory" just after his death :

" I was honoured with the friendly notice of Sir
Hudson Lowe, and enjoyed much of his confidence
during a course of thirty years. I knew him when his
military reputation marked him as an officer of the
highest promise ; I witnessed his able conduct as
Governor of St. Helena ; I saw him when the malice
of his enemies had gained the ascendant, and covered

[1] Rear-Admiral Sir George Cockburn took Napoleon to St.
Helena on the *Northumberland*, and was entrusted with his safe
custody until the arrival of Sir Hudson Lowe.

[2] From a letter of Sir George Bingham to Sir Hudson Lowe.

him with unmerited opprobrium ; I beheld him on his deathbed : and throughout these various phases of his career I admired and respected his character, while I truly loved the man. I knew him to be a kind, indulgent, affectionate husband and parent, a warm and steady friend, a placable, nay, generous enemy, and an upright public servant."[1]

This is a testimonial of which any man might be proud, and if Sir Hudson Lowe had died on the day he was appointed Governor of St. Helena the sentiments here expressed would have been received with universal applause. And yet we are asked to believe, on the authority of Mr. Barry O'Meara and some of Napoleon's fellow-exiles, that the character of Sir Hudson Lowe was as nearly as possible the reverse of all this! That he was mean, jealous, suspicious, tyrannical, utterly wanting in kindness and courtesy, fit only to be a jailer or a hangman !

Lord Rosebery has done his best to revive this tradition. "We are afraid," he says, "we must add that he was not what we should call, in the best sense, a gentleman. But a Government, which had wished Napoleon to be hanged or shot, was not likely to select any person of large or generous nature to watch over the remainder of his life ; nor, indeed, had they sought one, were they likely to secure one for such a post."[2]

[1] "United Service Magazine," March, 1844, p. 417.
[2] "Napoleon: the Last Phase," p. 66.

Placing this by the side of the testimonies to Sir Hudson Lowe's character we have just seen, we do not seem to be referring to the same individual. One of the greatest—if not the greatest—orators of antiquity gives a salutary piece of advice in forming a judgement upon a man's guilt or innocence : " In all cases," he says, " that are serious and important we must weigh the wishes, the intentions, the actions of the accused, not by the charge made against him, but by his previous character. For no one of us can be moulded in a moment, nor can a man's way of life be changed or his disposition altered on a sudden." [1] Surely then, before a shred of evidence upon Sir Hudson Lowe's conduct at St. Helena is heard on one side or the other, we have here a psychological puzzle of no ordinary difficulty.

[1] Cicero, "pro Sulla," § 69.

CHAPTER V

THE PLACE OF EXILE

Position of Napoleon.—Choice of St. Helena.—Climate of St. Helena.—Choice of Sir Hudson Lowe as Governor.

A GREAT mass of literature has accumulated round the events of Napoleon's exile at St. Helena, and it would be a hopeless task to attempt to deal with it in detail, or with all the charges that have been brought against Sir Hudson Lowe. I must therefore select a few of the most striking, and point out how easily they can be refuted. What is really difficult is to clear away the dense clouds of prejudice and misrepresentation that still envelop the memory of Sir Hudson Lowe and all that concerns him. However, before dealing with the evidence, such as it is, it is necessary to consider the circumstances altogether, and the aims and objects of those on whose testimony Sir Hudson Lowe has been condemned.

Napoleon always contended that he gave himself up only as the guest of the British nation, and he claimed their hospitality as such. He therefore regarded it as an act of tyranny and injustice that he should be treated as a prisoner or in any other way than as a guest. But this view cannot be maintained.

Two things must be borne in mind as established by the clearest evidence. The first, that Napoleon at the time he dictated his famous letter to the Prince Regent on the 13th of July, declaring that he had come to seek the hospitality of the British nation, could not, humanly speaking, have escaped to America or elsewhere; the second, that Captain Maitland, of the *Bellerophon*, undertook merely to convey Napoleon to England, and informed him through Las Cases "that he must consider himself entirely at the disposal of his Royal Highness the Prince Regent." Lord Rosebery says that had Napoleon "acted with promptitude he had reasonable chances of escaping to America."[1] If he had acted *with promptitude* he would have had, it is true, some chance, but it was a desperate chance; for, in consequence of rumours that Napoleon intended to attempt such an escape, English cruisers had been watching Rochefort for some time past, and on the 8th of July Admiral Hotham, on the *Superb*, wrote from Quiberon Bay to Maitland, then off Rochefort, that he was to use every exertion to intercept Napoleon should he try to escape. Even such slender chance as he may have had was stopped by Napoleon's own overtures, through Savary and Las Cases, to Maitland, on the 10th, for a pass to America. Maitland after that took care to make escape by sea impossible. As to the second point, Las Cases afterwards admitted the correctness of Maitland's state-

[1] "Napoleon: the Last Phase," p. 111.

ment, and no controversy could ever have arisen had Maitland taken the precaution (as he should have done in a matter of such importance) to give his answer in writing and to require the signature of Las Cases to it.[1] Dr. Holland Rose has given a clear and minute account of these transactions, and concludes with the just observation : " A man who is driven into a corner, and then comes forth with an appeal to the generosity of his foes, is as really a prisoner as if he were captured."[2] These facts have a most important bearing on the whole subject, for those who consider that the captivity was initiated in fraud will readily believe that it was continued in tyranny and persecution.

Napoleon then had no option but to surrender, if he wished to escape a worse fate. There was no hope for him. If he was still to live he might take one of three courses. He might have put himself at the head of the army at the Loire for a short period (but only to be killed or captured); he might have let himself be made prisoner; or he might have surrendered to one or other of his foes. The last course, the one which he actually adopted, was also the best for himself. He

[1] Mr. T. E. Watson says ("Napoleon," p. 673): "The entire episode reeks with dishonour. . . . It seems a shocking thing to open one's door to a vanquished foe, after he has knocked thereon with the plea of a guest; and then after having let him enter as a guest to bar the doors upon him as a prisoner." True enough if Napoleon *had* been allowed to enter as a guest, but, in the light of fact, this is the emptiest rhetoric.

[2] "Owens College Historical Essays," p. 502.

afterwards said he regretted he had not surrendered to the Emperor of Russia or the Emperor of Austria. Possibly, for a time, he did have this regret. We cannot of course say what would have happened in that case, but he would scarcely have surrendered to the King of Prussia, for Blücher had publicly declared that he would have had him shot over the grave of the Duc d'Enghien. It is idle then to pretend that he came as a guest on board the *Bellerophon*. The circumstances were very different from what they were a year before, when Napoleon had been allowed to take the sovereignty of Elba. He had returned to France, and it was now evident that no terms could bind him. It is true that Louis XVIII. had very shabbily neglected to pay Napoleon at Elba the instalments of the 2,000,000 francs per annum that had been agreed upon, and both the Russian Emperor and our envoy, Castlereagh, reproached Talleyrand for this conduct, but that had no connexion with Napoleon's escape from Elba. The question now was what was to be done with the ex-Emperor.

At that time Napoleon was not regarded with the sentimental interest which now attaches to his name and fate. There was hardly a household in the United Kingdom that could not point to the loss of some one at least of its members through the long continuance of the Great War, for which they primarily held the ambition of Napoleon responsible. If a man is able to become a world-conqueror, if he feels within himself the powers of an Alexander or a Caesar, we do not particularly blame him for exerting his powers. It is pedantic to put such a man on the level of a common malefactor because in the course of his career he has caused the death of thousands. If, however, his rewards are above those of ordinary people, so also are his risks ; and if in the end he fails, one cannot blame ordinary people for keeping him down by any means they can. Ordinary people wish to be let alone to play their modest part in life, and they resent the periodical clearing of the stage in order to exhibit the exploits of genius at their expense. For want of a better name Napoleon was called a " prisoner of war "; but every one knew that he was not to be treated precisely as a prisoner of war was usually treated. Common sense at any rate was on the side of the Lord Chancellor (Lord Eldon) when he gave it as his opinion "that the case was not provided for by anything to be found in Grotius or Vattel, but that the law of self-preservation would justify the keeping of Napoleon under restraint in some distant region, where he should be treated with all indulgence compatible with a due regard for the peace of mankind."

It has been asserted that St Helena was fixed upon as the place of Napoleon's detention at the Congress of Vienna, and that it was intended to transfer him thither from Elba.[1] Something of this kind seems to

[1] See Rosebery, p. 62. Lord Holland in his "Foreign Reminiscences," p. 196, states that the Government had been treat-

have got into the newspapers, but there is no record of it in the official proceedings of the Congress, and the Duke of Wellington denied that it was ever mentioned there.[1] As soon, however, as Napoleon's surrender appeared to be imminent, we find Lord Liverpool writing to Lord Castlereagh: "If we get possession of Napoleon's person we incline to the Cape of Good Hope or St Helena"; and he gives as a reason for choosing St. Helena that it was "the only place from which neutrals could be excluded without inconvenience,"[2] inasmuch as it was a possession of the East India Company. It was also recommended by the advisers of the Admiralty as being particularly healthy, and their decision was reinforced by a memorandum from General Alexander Beatson, a former Governor of the island, who recommended it because of its remoteness, its difficulty of access, and, on the other hand, the ease with which the approach of vessels could be signalled.[3]

At the time of Napoleon's surrender, an exile to

ing with the East India Company for the cession of St. Helena *early in* 1815; but that is inconsistent with the contemporary letters of Liverpool to Castlereagh. See "Owens College Historical Essays," p. 503 n.

[1] The Duke at a later period said. "St Helena was first suggested, I rather think, about the time when Elba was fixed upon" (Stanhope's "Notes of Conversations with the Duke of Wellington," p 105).

[2] Yonge's "Life of Lord Liverpool," ii 196.

[3] See the memorandum set out at length by Dr. Holland Rose in "Owens College Historical Essays," p. 504.

St. Helena or elsewhere was considered very lenient treatment, for there was then, as Sir Walter Scott reminds us, a considerable party in England who were in favour of handing him over to the Government of Louis XVIII. It is true that the Opposition in Parliament professed their horror at the measure dealt out to Napoleon, but that was merely because they were the Opposition ; and if they had been in power they could hardly have resisted the will of the nation, which demanded some measure of the sort, and readily acquiesced in the banishment to St. Helena. When then Napoleon considered it an outrage that he should be banished to St. Helena at all, the personality of the Governor was a minor matter. As Las Cases wrote in a suppressed passage of his journal : "The details of St. Helena are unimportant : to be there at all is the great grievance."[1]

The first thing charged against the British Government is the climate of St. Helena.[2] It is "common form" with many French writers to assume that the chief object the British Government had in sending Napoleon there was that he might be "assassinated" by the climate, which (they professed to think) would kill him in a few years. I verily believe this is the

[1] "Les détails de Ste.-Hélène sont peu de chose; c'est d'y être qui est la grande affaire."

[2] The climate of St. Helena is only discussed for the sake of completeness. No one at the present day disputes its healthiness.

G

only charge made on behalf of the Emperor in which
Sir Hudson Lowe is not involved, for it was not quite
asserted that he had the powers of Prospero. All
medical testimony is distinctly opposed to the notion
that St. Helena is unhealthy, the death-rate being
remarkably low. "For a tropical climate, only fifteen
degrees from the Line, St. Helena is certainly a healthy
island," writes Mr. Henry, "if not the most healthy of
this description in the world. During one period of
twelve months, we did not lose one man by disease
out of four hundred of the 66th quartered at Deadwood
[the camp near Longwood]." [1] But this point is hardly
worth labouring, because Las Cases says in his journal
that Napoleon remarked to him : "After all, as a place
of exile, perhaps St. Helena was the best. In high
latitudes we should have suffered greatly from cold,
and in any other island of the tropics we should have
expired miserably under the scorching rays of the
sun. This rock is wild and barren no doubt ; the
climate is monstrous and unwholesome ; but the tem-
perature, it must be confessed, is mild." [2] In accordance with the curious fatality that attends the charges
brought in connexion with the exile of Napoleon, we
have French evidence as to the desirability of St.
Helena as a place in which to settle. In a report
published in 1804 at Paris, *by order of the First Consul*,
St. Helena was called a terrestrial paradise, where the

[1] "Events of a Military Life," ii. 45.
[2] Las Cases' "Journal," February 1st, 1816.

air was pure and the sky serene, where health shone in every countenance, and diseases contracted in India were immediately cured. Finally, to bring the climate of St. Helena up to date, I quote the following passage from a prize essay on St. Helena by one of the Boer prisoners lately confined there.[1] He writes :

"This island has certainly reason to congratulate itself on the superb climate with which it has been blessed. Broadly speaking, the climate is steady and thoroughly reliable, it very seldom goes into extremes. It is very seldom broiling hot or freezing cold, rain never falls in torrents, nor are devastating tornadoes usual. Surrounded by the Atlantic, in the course of the trade-winds, this island has a cool, invigorating, and healthy climate."

To select an officer upon whom should be laid the responsibility for the safe custody of Napoleon was no easy matter for the British Government, and that they appointed Sir Hudson Lowe shows the high opinion they had formed of his vigilance, conscientiousness, and general ability. He was known, says Mr. Julian Corbett,[2] as a stern disciplinarian, a master of foreign languages, and as devoted to hard work. A

[1] Published in the "National Review" of October, 1902.

[2] In his article "Colonel Wilks and Napoleon" in the "Monthly Review," January, 1901, since separately published by Mr. Murray.

man who had attained to his position solely by his own merits must have been, as he remarks, "no vulgar martinet." If he were unduly suspicious, surely that was a fault, if a fault at all, on the right side. It was want of suspicion on the part of Sir Neil Campbell that had enabled Napoleon to escape from Elba, and a repetition of that *fiasco* had to be rendered impossible in any event. The Under-Secretary of State in the War Department, Sir Henry Bunbury, was a man of influence and had long been a friend of Sir Hudson Lowe. It was through him that Lowe had been appointed to the command in the south of France, and it was probably through him that Lowe was now appointed to have charge of Napoleon, though I am not aware of any decisive authority for this.[1] The Duke of Wellington would have preferred that Colonel Wilks,[2] the then Governor, should remain in that capacity and have charge of Napoleon ; but possibly he was considered to be not of sufficiently high rank, and

[1] Sir Harris Nicolas states this as a fact, but gives no authority.

[2] See Stanhope's "Notes of Conversations with the Duke of Wellington, p. 326 : "The Duke said that he thought the Government had been mistaken in removing the old East India Company Governor, Colonel Wilks He was a very intelligent, well-read man, and knew everything that had been passing in Europe, and Napoleon had become really attached to him. After he was gone, Napoleon (as the Duke mentions) said more than once 'Pourquoi n'ont-ils pas laissé ce vieux gouverneur ? Avec lui je me serais arrangé, nous n'aurions pas eu de querelles.'"

may have been thought too much of a courtier. As a fact, however, he pleased Napoleon, who would have liked him to remain, while at the same time he showed sufficient firmness in his conduct.

Whatever other reasons there may have been for the appointment of Sir Hudson Lowe, the reason given by Lord Rosebery, that "a Government, which had wished Napoleon to be hanged or shot, was not likely to select any person of large or generous nature to watch over the remainder of his life," is not one that will occur to a fair-minded reader. It is true that, as Lord Rosebery remarks a few pages before, Liverpool had written to Castlereagh expressing a wish that Louis XVIII. would "hang or shoot" Napoleon, but in the passage before us this is transformed into the official wish of the Government, which is a very different matter.[1] Liverpool also writes to Castlereagh that if Napoleon were to be kept a prisoner it would be better for us to detain him than for any other Power, which would thus prevent him from being hanged or shot, and the protest of the Duke of Wellington against shooting Napoleon is on record.

I am by no means claiming that Sir Hudson Lowe was exempt from faults, and these faults I will endeavour to state later ; but, whatever his faults were, they were not those that have been generally attributed to him. It may be said fearlessly that the choice of Government was fully justified by the conduct of Sir

[1] "Napoleon: the Last Phase," pp. 58, 66.

Hudson Lowe in his arduous position, and that the unmerited obloquy cast upon him, and still clinging to his memory in the minds of many people, was the result of the campaign of calumny directed against him and of the efficient manner in which he carried out his trust. As he repeatedly said, the office was not one that he had sought; but when once it was offered to him he had too high a sense of duty to decline it. Sir Hudson Lowe had, as we have seen, high qualifications for the post. On the other hand, it cannot be denied that the service he had seen had happened to be such that the new Governor could scarcely be regarded by Napoleon as a *persona grata*, and of this the Emperor was not slow to remind him. For instance, Sir Hudson Lowe had been in command of the Corsican Rangers, a body of men whom Napoleon not unnaturally regarded as brigands and traitors to their country. He had at the close of the war received the submission of Toulon, the place from which at the beginning of the war Napoleon had driven the British, and where he had first made his mark as a military genius. Again, as we have seen, Sir Hudson Lowe had brought home the news of Napoleon's abdication, and had been knighted for that very service. All these circumstances were certainly personal arguments against the appointment of Sir Hudson Lowe.

CHAPTER VI

ST. HELENA EVIDENCE

The Napoleonic Legend.—Object of the French attendants.—
"La politique de Longwood."—Evidence of the French.—
Evidence of O'Meara.—Of Jackson, Henry, and Rous.—Char-
acter of Sir Hudson Lowe.

SO far, in writing on Sir Hudson Lowe, I have
adopted the chronological method, as many details of his life are little known to the public. Ther
would be no advantage in continuing this method in
dealing with St. Helena affairs. The life there and
the talks of Napoleon have been described over and
over again in many publications. I therefore treat this
period as a whole, and refer more particularly only to
such details as throw light on the motives and conduct
of the Governor and his opponents.

There is a Napoleonic history and there is a Napoleonic legend. If the two are kept distinct, and if the
Legend is recognized as the Legend there is no great
harm done; but it is the constant endeavour of the
Legend to pass itself off as the History—the Legend is,
in short, the history of what Napoleon ought to have
said and done. It might be put together into a fairly
interesting book and placed by the side (by way of

antithesis) of Archbishop Whately's " Historic Doubts
relating to Napoleon Bonaparte," unless perhaps we
may consider that such a book has already been
written in Mr. T. E. Watson's "Napoleon." The chief
architects of the Legend—as regards St. Helena—are
Las Cases and Montholon. As a fabricator, Montholon is perhaps the more artistic, but Las Cases
sometimes unfortunately contradicts him, which is
hardly " playing the game." Montholon's superiority
as an inventor was recognized by Napoleon himself.
The credit of the well-known story of how Napoleon's
sword was demanded on board the *Bellerophon*, and
how the white-headed Admiral bowed his head for
shame on hearing the Emperor's fiery refusal, is due
to Montholon.[1] The story shows the hand of a master
and certainly ought to be true. That Napoleon could
have escaped to America, but preferred to be received
as a guest by the British nation is another point in
the Legend, and the whole life of the Emperor at St.
Helena, as told by Las Cases and Montholon, is part
of it. Sometimes we can trace the progress from
history to legend. The Legend says that the death of
Napoleon was due to " chronic hepatitis," to use
O'Meara's phrase, caused by the climate of St. Helena.
When a *post mortem* examination revealed the fact
that death was due to cancer of the stomach, Montholon immediately wrote to his wife (who had then
left the island): " The opening of his body took place

[1] See above, p. 24 n.

this morning. It proved that he died of the same illness as his father, a *squirre ulcereuse* in the stomach,
near the pylorus. It is in our misfortune a great con-
solation for us to have obtained proof that his death
is not and cannot have been in any way the result of
his captivity or of the deprivation of all the cares that
perhaps Europe might have offered." [1] This statement
of fact, however, is too crude for the Legend. In after
years we find Montholon recurring in his book to the
climate story, or, as Lord Rosebery expresses it, " he
gallantly maintained the theory of a liver complaint." [2]
People not lost in admiration of the genius of Montholon might perhaps employ a less complimentary
adverb. Lord Rosebery's remark that " Napoleon at
St. Helena was, as it were, making the best case for
himself, just as he was in the habit of doing in his
bulletins," admits the Legend, but it cannot be allowed
that "at St. Helena his only practical aim was to further
the interests of his dynasty and his son, so that where
these are not directly concerned the memoirs may be
considered as somewhat more reliable than the bulletins." [3] The Legend had an even more practical object at this time, and that was to effect the Emperor's
own recall. For a long time the exiles confidently expected this, either through some revolution in France,

---

[1] See the letter quoted in the " Quarterly Review," March,
1848, also by Dr. Holland Rose in " Owens College Historical
Essays," p. 520.

[2] " Napoleon: the Last Phase," p. 220.   [3] *Ibid.*, p. 4.

or even from a mere change of Government in England. Thus, on the fourth interview of Sir Hudson Lowe with Napoleon, the latter said, in reply to some question about a house : " In a couple of years there will be a change in the Ministry in England, or a new Government in France, and I shall no longer be here." Napoleon evidently over-estimated the difference between the Government and the Opposition in the British Parliament. He thought that the speeches of the Opposition, merely made with the view of embarrassing their opponents, really expressed their convictions, and that if Lord Holland and his friends came into power he would speedily be recalled from exile, for almost from the first the treatment of Napoleon, like most other things, was made a party question. In accordance with this deliberate plan it was necessary that Napoleon and his grievances should be put before the European, and more especially the British, public, at any cost. " It was his business to have complaints," says Lockhart. The favourite Napoleonic maxim, " Policy justifies everything," was constantly in request at St. Helena, and the disciples did not fall short of their master in its application.

The conduct of Napoleon and his suite towards Sir Hudson Lowe was not therefore due merely to caprice or ill-temper,[1] but was the result of a carefully settled

---

[1] Lord Rosebery says that the French attendants were not guilty of *wanton* misrepresentations, etc., but no one ever thought they were.

plan by which they hoped to secure their very practical object.

"In pursuance of this system," says a writer in the "Hereford Journal," in 1853, no doubt Colonel Jackson, "all communications from Sir Hudson, written or otherwise, were to be misunderstood; points which it was well known to be out of the power of Sir Hudson to concede were to be perpetually insisted on; all acts of courtesy were to be construed into insults, every proposed amelioration of their condition was to be received as an aggravation of their misery, while lying to any extent was to be unscrupulously resorted to whenever it could forward the great end they had in view." Generals Bertrand, Montholon, and Gourgaud, and Count Las Cases were all honourable men—"at least according to the *Code Napoléon*," as Colonel Jackson caustically observes—and we need not bestow too much severity of censure on any of their acts in the service of a master whose will to them was law. Count Las Cases was a worshipper by nature; he said the Emperor was his god, and an eloquent French writer has said of him: "He had the servility of a domestic and the blindness of a devotee." Bertrand was, according to Mr. Henry,[1] who knew him well at St. Helena, the most honest and honourable man of the Longwood establishment, and, he adds, "*on all other subjects than those immediately relating to the Emperor's interests*, of unimpeachable veracity." This, however,

[1] "Events of a Military Life," ii. 92.

is rather a large deduction, considering that Bertrand said or did little at St. Helena that had not reference to the Emperor. Even among this party Count Montholon was distinguished for his disregard of truth.[1] An amusing instance of this is found in the statement in his "Récits"[2] of his regret at General Gourgaud's departure, when only a month before Gourgaud had challenged Montholon to a duel, which the latter declined only on the ground of his attendance on the Emperor! Montholon also wrote of Las Cases: "We all loved the well-informed and good man, whom we had pleasure in venerating as a Mentor. . . . He was an immense loss to us," though at St. Helena he tried to make the secretary's life miserable, and on one occasion predicted to Gourgaud that he would soon leave the island.[3] Of General Gourgaud I shall have more to say later. While at St. Helena he conducted himself with perfect propriety, which was probably one reason why he fell into the Emperor's bad graces. The evidence of the French, then, is of little account as against Sir Hudson Lowe; but their admissions are valuable as evidence in his favour. Now it happens

[1] Count Balmain says of him: "Il se croit un personnage et passe pour un menteur déterminé" (Balmain, p. 584).

[2] Vol. iii. p. 3 (English edition). See also Forsyth, ii. 248 and iii. 390. The date of the challenge was February 4th, 1818, and General Gourgaud embarked for England on March 14th. As a favour he was allowed to sail for Europe direct instead of going first to the Cape.

[3] See Rose's "Napoleon I.," ii. 560 n.

that we have these admissions in abundance. When Las Cases was sent away from St. Helena for misconduct, at the end of 1816, the MS. of his journal came into the hands of the Governor, who, before returning it, very properly had it copied as a matter of public interest. This journal contains many passages that are suppressed in the journal as published. One of the suppressed passages is as follows:

"We are possessed of moral arms only; and in order to make the most advantageous use of these it was necessary to reduce into *a system* our demeanour, our words, our sentiments, *even our privations*, in order that we might thereby excite a lively interest in a large portion of the population of Europe, and that the Opposition in England might not fail to attack the Ministry on the violence of their conduct towards us." [1]

Colonel Basil Jackson informs us [2] that while visiting Paris in 1828 he accidentally met Count Montholon, who invited his wife and himself to pass a few days at his country seat. Colonel Jackson thus continues:

[1] Under the date of November 30th, 1815. This passage is given by Forsyth, vol. i. p. 5. Lord Rosebery says of the suppressed passages: "If indeed they exist or ever existed" (p. 5). They are among the *Lowe* papers in the British Museum, which any holder of a reading-ticket can inspect for himself if he cares to take the trouble.

[2] "Waterloo and St. Helena," pp. 103 foll.

" He [Count Montholon] enlarged upon what he termed *la politique de Longwood*, spoke not unkindly of Sir Hudson Lowe, allowing he had a difficult task to execute, *since an angel from heaven as Governor could not have pleased them.* When I more than hinted that nothing could justify detraction and departure from truth in carrying out a policy, he merely shrugged his shoulders and reiterated, ' C'était notre politique, et que voulez-vous ? ' That he and the others respected Sir Hudson Lowe I had not the shadow of a doubt; nay, in a conversation with Montholon at St. Helena, when speaking of the Governor, he observed that Sir Hudson was an officer who would always have distinguished employment, as all governments were glad of the services of a man of his calibre. Happening to mention that, owing to his inability to find an officer who could understand and speak French, the Governor was disposed to employ me as orderly officer at Longwood, Montholon said it was well for me that I was not appointed to the post, as they did not want a person in that capacity who could understand them; in fact, he said, ' We should have found means to get rid of you, and perhaps ruined you.' Now, it was simply because an officer of the rank of captain had always acted at Longwood, and the Governor knew that to have sent them an officer who was only a lieutenant would have been deemed a kind of insult by Napoleon, and as such resented. I was subsequently glad the project failed."

These admissions require no comment, for, after all, it is superfluous to accuse of lying those who do not profess to speak the truth. Moreover, we have the evidence of O'Meara, who, writing to Sir Thomas Reade [1] on July 10th, 1816, while he was still on good terms with Sir Hudson Lowe, thus expresses himself: " They [the French] are sufficiently malignant to impute all these things [want of proper provisions] to the Governor, instead of setting them down as being owing to the neglect or carelessness of some of Balcombe's [the purveyor] people. Every little circumstance is carried directly to Bonaparte, with every aggravation that malignity and falsehood can suggest to evil-disposed and cankered minds." [2] It is needless to add that this passage does not occur in his published book.

We thus have a clue to guide us through all the plausible statements made by writers on behalf of Napoleon. There was a regular series of them. First, the publication of Warden, the surgeon of the *Northumberland*, then that of Santini, one of Napoleon's servants. Both these appeared in the Emperor's lifetime, and we have the advantage of his own comments on them. Of Warden's book he said: " The foundation of it is true; but in it there are *cento coglioniere e cento bugie* (a hundred absurdities and a hundred lies)."

---

[1] The Deputy Adjutant-General. A French publication spoke of him as *Le Castlereagh de Ste.-Hélène.* Count Balmain calls him *un John Bull tout cru.*

[2] Forsyth, i. 237.

But this is speaking too gently. General Gourgaud wrote of it as a " mere tissue of falsehoods." Of Santini's book (which, as it turned out, was not by Santini at all) Napoleon said that it was " a foolish production, exaggerated, full of *coglioniere* and some lies." There were also " Letters from the Cape," in reply to Warden, which were probably dictated by Napoleon himself, and the " Manuscrit venu de Ste.-Hélène d'une manière inconnue," the *provenance* of which is uncertain. However, these brochures served their purpose, which was to gull the British public. Las Cases' journal is of course a more serious publication ; but the published journal, as above remarked, is very different from the MS. journal that came into the hands of Sir Hudson Lowe. Other publications were the " Recueil de pièces authentiques sur le captif de Ste.-Hélène," in twelve volumes, and at a much later period the " Récits " of Montholon. The most influential book, however, was O'Meara's " Voice from St. Helena," of which I must speak more particularly. There seems to have been no personal animosity on the part of the French towards Sir Hudson Lowe. Like Lady Teazle, they took away his character with the utmost good-nature. This is shown, not only by their own admissions afterwards, but also by their conduct immediately after the death of Napoleon. " The hatchet was buried," and Counts Bertrand and Montholon (Las Cases and Gourgaud having left St. Helena long before) made their peace with Sir Hudson

Lowe, who, with his accustomed generosity, was quite willing to meet them. They all called at the Governor's house, stayed to lunch, and dined there on the following day. There was no reason for keeping up appearances any longer. We have similar testimony from Colonel Jackson, who wrote thus to Mr. Forsyth:

" I never heard any of the French say a word against Sir Hudson Lowe's bearing towards them. His orders to his officers were to do all that courtesy and kindness could dictate to render the situation of the French persons as little unpleasant as possible, and, so far as I saw, every desire on their part was promptly attended to. He was himself a man possessing little of what is called *manner*—no man had less of that—but he was full of kindness, liberality, and consideration for the feelings of others." [1]

Thus, when Count Bertrand's house was being built near Longwood, the Countess wished a verandah to be added, says Colonel Jackson. What was the stern and cruel reply of the Governor?—" By all means," he said, " have a verandah erected." " From one thing to another," continues Jackson, " the verandah became a good-sized room, and I used to compliment the Countess on her cleverness in verandah planning." [2] We find the same lady returning thanks for a donkey which the Governor sent for her little boy, and for a

[1] Forsyth, i. 135 n.
[2] " Waterloo and St. Helena," p. 130.

H

picture in tapestry which had been detained from her by a person in the island, and which the Governor instantly procured for her. "These are trifles in themselves," says Mr. Forsyth, "but they are trifles which indicate kindness; and a man's disposition and character are often more clearly shown in little things than in matters of more serious import." From this absence of personal feeling we must probably except Count Las Cases, who certainly seems to have cherished some spite against Sir Hudson Lowe. At any rate, his son did, as we shall see later. For some time before his death Napoleon himself, perceiving that his hopes of recall were entirely baseless, seems to have become more reconciled to his lot, and really to have shown some gratitude for the constant attentions shown him by Sir Hudson Lowe On his deathbed he charged Bertrand and Montholon to seek a reconciliation with the Governor, which was done with the result above mentioned. The tragi-comedy of five years was played out.

It must be allowed that Napoleon was less difficult to deal with than his attendants. Affairs might have been more readily adjusted if more personal intercourse between the Governor and his illustrious captive had taken place. But they only had five interviews in all,[1] and the last of them was only four

[1] Not including the short interview of June 20th, 1816, which was merely for the purpose of introducing to Napoleon the new Admiral, Sir Pulteney Malcolm.

months after Sir Hudson Lowe's arrival. It was, as we have seen, Bertrand, Montholon, and others who persistently and purposely exaggerated and misrepresented everything, in order to make occasions of quarrel. This was, in short, *la politique de Longwood.*

The complaints of the French writers are such as might be expected from the circumstances in which they were placed, and naturally, owing to those circumstances, would not make much impression on an impartial reader. Moreover, their own admissions have sufficiently discounted the value of their evidence. There is another person whose statements and insinuations have been, we may say, almost the only cause in England of the odium cast upon Sir Hudson Lowe. I refer to Napoleon's surgeon, Mr. Barry O'Meara. We have seen what manner of man Sir Hudson Lowe was. Let us also examine the character of Mr. Barry O'Meara, and when that is fully appreciated the most difficult part of my task will be accomplished. One cannot be surprised at the amount of prejudice raised against Sir Hudson Lowe by the " Voice from St. Helena." It is written with an engaging air of frankness —" an affected candour," says Colonel Jackson—and considerable literary skill, and would naturally lead the reader into the belief of the account given therein. Besides, it seemed unlikely, to say the least, that a British officer would so far forget his position and his duty as to enlist himself secretly in Napoleon's service, to become *l'homme de l'Empereur,* as the phrase was, and therefore to misstate facts deliberately for the purpose of producing sympathy for Napoleon. And again, if a British officer were willing to be guilty of such treachery, there did not seem to be sufficient inducement for it. But these two unlikely things turned out to be strictly true. O'Meara was guilty of this baseness, he had sufficient inducement, and he received the reward which he had certainly earned. Barry O'Meara was surgeon on board the *Bellerophon* when Napoleon surrendered to Captain Maitland. He recommended himself to the Emperor's notice, and was subsequently asked to become his surgeon. It is not necessary to suppose, in the first instance, anything further than that O'Meara succumbed to the fascination of the Emperor. There is abundant testimony to the great personal attraction which Napoleon exercised over those with whom he came into contact. How great this attraction was may be inferred from a remark of Admiral Lord Keith, who, in reply to repeated applications on behalf of Napoleon for a personal interview with the Prince Regent, exclaimed: "That would never do! In half an hour they would be excellent friends!" Gourgaud's "Journal," however, reveals the fact that at a later period O'Meara received money from the Emperor.[1]

As the Emperor's surgeon, O'Meara sailed to St. Helena on board the *Northumberland*, and was in per-

[1] See Gourgaud's "Journal," October 4th, 1817, quoted in Rose's "Napoleon I.," ii 565.

sonal attendance upon Napoleon afterwards until his
summary removal by the order of the Government in
the middle of 1818. Being a man of plausibility and
considerable social gifts, he managed for some time to
keep on good terms both with Napoleon and with Sir
Hudson Lowe, and *spontaneously* gave to the latter a
good deal of information of how matters were going
at Longwood. The Governor, in fact, procured the
raising of his salary from £365 to £520. Sir Hudson
Lowe, however, was naturally unwilling to question
O'Meara on this delicate subject, as it might be
thought he wished the surgeon to act as a spy—until
he ascertained that O'Meara was in the habit of carrying on a detailed correspondence with a friend at the
Admiralty, and then he considered that what was of
sufficient importance to be conveyed direct to England
for the benefit of the Cabinet—for this correspondence
was shown to them—certainly ought to be communicated to himself. Even then the Governor left it to
O'Meara to say what he chose, and to select what was
proper to be thus communicated. And yet O'Meara
had the impudence to charge the Governor with wishing to employ him as a spy! This charge against Sir
Hudson Lowe has unfortunately met with much belief. For instance, the writer of the notice of O'Meara
in the "Dictionary of National Biography" says:
"Lowe wished him to act to some extent as a spy
upon his prisoner and to repeat to him the private
conversation of the Emperor." No doubt Admiral

Malcolm considered there was a system of spying, but this will be dealt with later. We are now dealing with O'Meara, and for the statement in the "Dictionary" just quoted we have only O'Meara's word. Let us hear Sir Hudson himself. In a private letter to Lord Bathurst, soon after O'Meara's enforced departure, the Governor entered into the question of his conduct towards that person. He said:

"There are three points upon which I have conceived Mr. O'Meara may endeavour to raise a voice in his favour.

"*First*, he may say I wanted to employ him as a spy. *Answer:* I never asked him to give me any other information than what he had been in the habit of carrying to Sir George Cockburn, and this I asked him even in Sir George's presence; since when even Count Montholon has acknowledged I had a right to expect being informed of any discussions into which he might enter with General Bonaparte respecting my duties or his own, or of any improper communications going on.

"*Secondly*, he may ask why, if I had complaints against him, I did not bring them to a hearing. *Answer:* The complaints against him were of such a nature as that, if proved, I could not have suffered him to remain on the island without the worst effect of example, from a supposed impunity, upon the officers and inhabitants in general; and having received his resignation, reporting to Government General Bonaparte's application for a French or Italian physician to succeed him, I considered it best, unless he should himself apply to the Admiral, to let matters rest until the answer of Government should be received. [That is, an answer to a representation made by Sir Hudson Lowe about Mr. O'Meara's conduct.]

" *Thirdly*, he may complain of my general mode of treatment towards him. *Answer:* If, through consideration to the very particular circumstances of General Bonaparte's situation, I was induced to act with a moderation and apparent lenity towards Mr. O'Meara which I could not have done towards any other individual, this was no reason I should at the same time continue to him those personal regards as an officer and a gentleman which his conduct and proceedings had appeared to me to destroy all claim to. I never, therefore, suffered him to enter my house, except by the outer door of it, which leads to the Secretary's office; and whenever he attempted to manifest any impertinence in his replies to my interrogatories, dismissed him immediately from my presence."

It may be questioned whether it would not have been better to hear the complaints against O'Meara judicially in order for the Governor to put himself right with European opinion for depriving the Emperor of the surgeon's services. Count Balmain certainly thought so.[1] However, as we shall see directly, O'Meara was

[1] Balmain, p. 681.

sent home by order of the Government, not by Sir Hudson Lowe.

But O'Meara was not only untrue to his salt, he was guilty of a double treachery, for at the very time when he was giving some information to Sir Hudson Lowe and much more to his friend at the Admiralty (Mr. Finlaison) he had actually long been under a pledge to Napoleon himself "not to reveal the conversations that passed between them, unless they related to his escape." Mr. O'Meara, having already made shipwreck of his own honour, tried to induce others to follow his example. I have already had occasion to refer to Mr. Walter Henry, who was at this time at St. Helena as assistant-surgeon, and soon as acting-surgeon, of the 66th Regiment. In his very interesting work, " Events of a Military Life," he devotes about one hundred pages to his experiences on the island. Not a word has ever been uttered against his character, and his narrative is amply confirmed in its details by the letters and official documents which Mr. Forsyth has published. Mr. Henry gives an account of how an attempt was made to bribe him to become *l'homme de l'Empereur* through the agency of O'Meara. He had attended Cipriani, the *maître d'hôtel* of Napoleon, during an illness which proved fatal, and he was asked through O'Meara to accept a breakfast service of plate. He describes in an amusing way the visions he had of this present, but the British Parliament had lately made the acceptance of any gift from Napoleon a criminal act, and his duty was clear. "The matter," he says, "was plain enough—a palpable attempt at a bribe, to enlist even so humble a person as myself into Napoleon's service, and to bind him down to implicit obedience, by first making him commit himself in a wrong action." It was a case of this sort, another attempt to bribe in which O'Meara acted the part of an intermediary, that led to restrictions being laid on him by the Governor in April, 1818. However, the account of Mr. Forsyth is much too lengthy and minute, so I will quote the narrative of Mr. Henry, every word of which is amply confirmed by documentary evidence.

"Mr. O'Meara, on finding his intrigues with the persons he had tried to bribe discovered, sent in his resignation; whilst at the same time Napoleon applied for a foreign medical attendant. Sir Hudson Lowe sent home their applications, confining Mr. O'Meara to the bounds of Longwood, and placing him under the same restrictions as the other persons of Napoleon's household. A few weeks after this an order arrived from England to send home Mr. O'Meara; not from any representations from Sir Hudson Lowe—for there was not time for the recent offence of this gentleman to be communicated—but in consequence of information received by the Government at home inculpating him as the tool of the fallen Emperor."[1]

[1] Henry, ii. pp. 40, 41.

This information related to clandestine correspondence, and had been given by General Gourgaud, who had recently returned from St. Helena. It is important to observe that it was the Government and not Sir Hudson Lowe who removed Mr. O'Meara.[1] Sir Hudson Lowe had not had up to this time proof of O'Meara's complicity, and the way in which the latter was backed up by influential members of the Government had prevented the Governor from taking all the steps he might otherwise have taken. However, very soon after O'Meara's departure there arrived at St. Helena such convincing proof of his being a tool of the Emperor as amply justified the Government in their action. After April, 1818, but before the summary order for his dismissal had been received, O'Meara was excluded from the mess of the 66th Regiment, of which he had been an honorary member. Of course he has set this down entirely to the machinations of the wicked Governor. In his book he attributes it to Sir Hudson Lowe's having employed Sir Thomas Reade to fill the mind of Colonel Lascelles with the most insidious calumnies against him, and to insinuate that his expulsion would be very agreeable to the Governor. As this is a good example of O'Meara's misrepresentations, I will give the particulars of it

[1] There was much unnecessary secrecy about this matter at the time, which was unwise of the Governor. Count Balmain says: "It is unknown at St. Helena what has decided Lord Bathurst to take away his employment" (Balmain, p. 684).

from the narrative of Mr. Henry, who was in a position to know accurately what happened. It is true that O'Meara was excluded from the mess, that it was due to the intervention of Sir Hudson Lowe, and that some of the officers of the mess expressed their regret at his departure. However, let us hear Mr. Henry, and we can then judge whether Mr. O'Meara had much ground for complaint. He writes as follows:

"About this time Mr. O'Meara, having been discovered tampering with two or three individuals on the island, with the object of prevailing on them to accept presents clandestinely from Napoleon, in violation of the regulations in force; and being also accused of repeating the confidential conversation of our mess, of which he was an honorary member, at Longwood, the Governor stated the facts of the case to Sir George Bingham and to the Commanding Officer of the 66th, intimating to the latter his opinion that Mr. O'Meara should not be permitted to continue a member of the mess, he having abused the privileges his position gave him. . . . Without consulting the officers of the mess, or submitting for their consideration the facts communicated to him by the Governor, the Commanding Officer sent a written intimation to Mr. O'Meara that his society was no longer desired by the regiment, which pretty strong hint the doctor disregarded, came to dinner the same day, and afterwards appealed to the officers of the mess as to the propriety of his conduct whilst mixing with them. Having been kept in the dark as to the real culpability of Mr. O'Meara, and being, perhaps, a little piqued at the proceedings of their Commanding Officer, they readily certified to the gentlemanly deportment of Mr. O'Meara whilst he was a member of the mess. . . . It is, I think, much to be regretted that the officers of the 66th should have given Mr. O'Meara any written certificate of good conduct whilst a member of their mess. However correct his behaviour might have been before, the gross insult to our Commanding Officer, and indirectly to ourselves, of sitting down to dinner after the prohibitory note he had received ought to have prevented any verbal or written testimony being given to a man who could act with such effrontery. As it turned out, our certificate eventually became one chief prop to the credibility of O'Meara's 'Voice from St. Helena'—a specious but sophistical book, full of misrepresentations, yet more remarkable for the *suppressio veri* than the *assertio falsi*. . . . With reference to the breach of social confidence in reporting our mess conversation to Bonaparte, I have no doubt whatever of the fact. In the unreserve of conversation with Madame Bertrand on the voyage to England, after the death of Napoleon, she acknowledged to me that this charge was true."[1]

Immediately after his arrival in England O'Meara addressed a long letter to the Admiralty in self-

[1] Henry, ii. pp. 40, 41.

justification, full of complaints against Sir Hudson Lowe. However, he overreached himself, and, intending murder, committed suicide, for he introduced into it the monstrous insinuation that the Governor had sounded him as to his willingness to hasten the death of the Emperor by artificial means.[1] The reply from the Secretary to the Admiralty was short and obvious. It contained these words:

"There is one passage in your said letter of such a nature as to supersede the necessity of animadverting upon any other parts of it. This passage is as follows [the passage containing the above insinuation is then set out]. It is impossible to doubt the meaning which this passage was intended to convey, and my Lords can as little doubt that the insinuation is a calumnious falsehood, but if it were true, and if so horrible a suggestion were made to you directly or indirectly, it was your bounden duty not to have lost a moment in communicating it to the Admiral on the spot, or to the Secretary of State, or to their Lordships.

"An overture so monstrous in itself, and so deeply involving not merely the personal character of the Governor, but the honour of the nation and the important

[1] On this alleged design to poison Napoleon, Count Montholon made a characteristic remark. "We don't believe it ourselves, *but it is always a useful thing to say*" ("Nous ne le croyons pas nous-mêmes, *mais c'est toujours bon à dire*"). The malignity of the charge is hardly greater than its absurdity (Forsyth, iii. 187 n.).

interests committed to his charge, should not have been reserved in your own breast for two years, to be produced at last, not (as it would appear) from a sense of public duty, but in furtherance of your personal hostility against the Governor.

"Either the charge is in the last degree false and calumnious, or you can have no possible excuse for having hitherto suppressed it. In either case, and without adverting to the general tenor of your conduct as stated in your letter, my Lords consider you to be an improper person to continue in His Majesty's service, and they have directed your name to be erased from the list of Naval Surgeons accordingly.—I have, etc.

(Signed) "J. W. CROKER."

This then is the man whose "Voice from St. Helena" has been republished so recently as 1888! This is the man who has been immortalized by Byron in the well-known couplet:

> And the stiff surgeon who maintained his cause
> Hath lost his place and gained the world's applause.

Of which two lines it is sufficient to say that they contain about as much truth as O'Meara's own statements. The dismissal of course put an end to O'Meara's public career; but if his activity was limited in one direction, there were other fields open. He could still calumniate, and his efforts in this direction, we must admit, were crowned with well-deserved success. In

1822 he brought out in two volumes "A Voice from St. Helena"—a book with an attractive title, an agreeable style, and the other characteristics I have before mentioned. It had an immense literary success, five editions being run through in a few months. What caused its popularity was not the report of Napoleon's conversations but the unscrupulous attack upon Sir Hudson Lowe, for the literature of detraction has never wanted a fit audience. Tacitus tells us that he deliberately began his "Annals" with the principate of Tiberius, in order to depict the Roman Empire in the blackest colours. If I may compare small things with great, O'Meara dipped his pen in gall to show us Sir Hudson Lowe as the Tiberius of St. Helena —and he has had his reward. Has he not been embalmed in a couplet? Was he not pensioned by the Bonaparte family, admitted to the affections of a rich old lady as a third husband (her first marriage was nine years before the birth of O'Meara), and again pensioned by her, besides being, as Mr. Henry says, " admired, quoted, and panegyrised by all the Bonapartists yet extant"? Is not this enough to atone for the brutality of a dozen Sir Hudson Lowes? And yet the writer of the memoir of O'Meara—prefixed to the recent edition of his book—speaks of his " disappointed hopes"! Really, he must have been hard to please.

One result of O'Meara's popularity among the Bonapartists, however, must not be omitted. It is a remarkable example of the irony of life. After the establish-

ment of the second empire, the mother of that excellent
and pious lady, the late Miss Kathleen O'Meara, the
authoress of the "Life of Ozanam" and many charming works of fiction, was, it seems, awarded a handsome pension on the ground of being the daughter-
in-law of that self-convicted calumniator, Mr. Barry
O'Meara! I say "self-convicted," for it is a singular
fact in connexion with the exile of Napoleon at St.
Helena that most of the charges made against Sir
Hudson Lowe can be disproved by the evidence of
the very people who made them. What supplies the
poison also supplies the antidote. We have seen how
Napoleon's suite admitted that the whole of their conduct was based on a system, and when that system
necessarily came to an end on the death of Napoleon
they acknowledged they had nothing to say against
the Governor. So in the case of O'Meara. He was
carrying on a correspondence with his friend Mr. Finlaison at the Admiralty, and the garbled accounts
afterwards concocted for "A Voice from St. Helena"
are often in point blank contradiction to the accounts
written at the time when the events narrated took
place! It has been the business of Mr. Forsyth in
his work to go minutely into this, and to confront
O'Meara in page after page of his book with his own
statements made in letters at the time. O'Meara's
character was thoroughly exposed in the "Quarterly
Review" for October, 1822, and to this he had the
prudence not to make any reply. A few years after

the death of Sir Hudson Lowe, Mr. Murray commissioned Sir Harris Nicolas, the well-known antiquary, to prepare for publication the papers of the late Governor of St. Helena, as has been mentioned before. Unfortunately, Sir Harris Nicolas died before completing his task, but the opinion he had formed of some of the persons involved is expressed in two letters to Colonel Jackson, who had furnished him with some information. He thus writes from Boulogne, March 1st, 1848, of Sir Hudson Lowe: "Not a spot will, I hope and believe, rest upon his memory. Such an exposure of lying, malignity, and scoundrelism on the part of O'Meara, Montholon, Las Cases, Antommarchi [the Italian surgeon], etc., as the work will exhibit, will be almost unprecedented." And again, on March 30th: "By the time I have finished I think I shall have been in company with *more liars* than any living author. If people meet in the next world with a knowledge of each other, and with an exposure of their several falsehoods and villany, what must have been the scenes between Sir Hudson Lowe, Las Cases, and O'Meara!"[1] The papers of Sir Hudson Lowe were subsequently put into the hands of Mr. Forsyth, who thus, in his preface, comments with just severity upon O'Meara:

"I am not one of those who think that conduct such as he has been guilty of in slandering others

[1] These letters are published in "Waterloo and St. Helena," pp. 181, 182.

may be sufficiently censured in the dulcet tones of gentle animadversion. He merits a sterner and more fearless judgement. Such writers are the pest of literature. They corrupt the stream of history by poisoning its fountains, and the effect of his work has been to mislead all succeeding authors and perpetuate a tale of falsehood."

He says further on, of O'Meara's book:

"The object of the 'Voice' was to avenge himself upon Sir Hudson Lowe, as the supposed author of his disgrace. And the means of accomplishing this were not difficult to a man who was content to sacrifice truth, honour, and honesty in the attempt. He had been in constant intercourse with Napoleon, and had had many confidential interviews with Sir Hudson Lowe. He knew perfectly well the real character of every alleged grievance and complaint, and he had taken copious notes of transactions and conversations as they occurred. What then was more easy than to recast these memoranda and garble them to suit the object he had in view—to suppress some passages and add others, so as to alter the tone and complexion of the original, and yet preserve throughout a substratum of fact? And this is what O'Meara has done. It is a serious charge to bring against a writer, and one which ought not to be lightly made nor readily believed. But, happily for the cause of truth, in this case, proofs, amounting to demonstration, of what is here asserted can be supplied."

Mr. Forsyth then refers to the series of confidential letters of O'Meara to Mr. Finlaison and to the notes of conversations made at the time by Major Gorrequer, the Governor's Military Secretary. Of Napoleon Mr. Forsyth says in his preface:

" If I know anything of myself, my sympathies were in his favour. I cannot now sufficiently express my admiration of his genius; but neither can I blind myself to the fact that he did not exhibit in misfortune that magnanimity without which there is no real greatness, and that he concentrated the energies of his mighty intellect on the ignoble task of insulting the Governor of St. Helena and manufacturing a case of hardship and oppression for himself. I have endeavoured to hold the balance even, and it is not the weight of prejudice, but of facts, which has made one of the scales preponderate."

Of Sir Hudson Lowe he writes : " I was not asked to make out a case for Sir Hudson Lowe, nor, had I been asked to do so, would I have consented. I regarded the duty of examining the papers left by him as a solemn trust, for the due and truthful discharge of which I was responsible to the public, and a still more searching tribunal, my own conscience."

I have already described the nature of the " Voice from St. Helena." I would gladly omit all mention of the republication in 1888; but as that book would now be given to any one inquiring for O'Meara's narrative, it is necessary to say a few words about it. It is handsomely got up, with excellent paper and print and some interesting illustrations, and has been rechristened " Napoleon at St. Helena." There are some additions and some omissions. The additional matter shows all the good intention of O'Meara without his literary ability. The book is introduced with a quotation (given twice over) from Carlyle, who says: " O'Meara's work has increased my respect for Napoleon "; and then goes on to compare Napoleon to Prometheus Vinctus, " arising above it all by the stern force of his own unconquerable spirit." Unconscious satire could hardly go further. Carlyle, after all, merely says (but expresses better) what any one who had read O'Meara's book *only* might say. It is obvious that he knew nothing of the other side, and therefore this is a mere *obiter dictum* of no value. Next come two short memoirs of Sir Hudson Lowe and Mr. O'Meara respectively, then a lengthy introduction. The writer on Sir Hudson Lowe in the " Dictionary of National Biography," to whom reference has already been made, shortly says of the " Lives" in this book that they are " worthless," an epithet which an examination amply confirms. Taking them with the introduction, it is not unjust to say that many of the " facts" are fiction, while the

method of argument shows an ineptitude of which
O'Meara (to do him justice) would have been ashamed.
One or two specimens will suffice. We read, in allusion
to Sir Hudson Lowe's delay in prosecuting O'Meara
for libel: "The only reason given by Lowe for his
delay was the time required for meeting charges in
which truth was so artfully blended with falsehood—
an admission that we have a good deal of truth in the
journal." Precisely; it is the truth mingled with the
falsehood that makes it so dangerous. Exaggeration
and misrepresentation of facts are always more difficult
to expose than pure fiction, and a book that spreads
these broadcast is proportionately more venomous and
deadly, for

> The lie that is half the truth is ever the blackest of lies.

Again, there is quoted, as a testimonial to O'Meara,
an extract from a letter of Lord Dudley (in the Dudley
Letters) to which he is certainly welcome. Having
met the author of the "Voice from St. Helena" at
dinner, Lord Dudley writes as follows:

"He is cheerful, good-humoured and communicative,
and, in spite of an air of confident vulgarity which is
diffused over all his behaviour, the impression he made
on me was rather favourable. At least my belief in
what he has told was strengthened by having seen
him, and still more so by some conversation which I
happened to have the very next day with Sir G——
C——, whom I met at Gloucester Lodge. He defends

Sir Hudson Lowe only just as far as prudence and decorum oblige an official man to do so. Indeed, he acknowledged that, with respect to what passed in St. Helena, he was disposed to take O'Meara's part. He mentioned a circumstance, however, since O'Meara's return to England, which he thought disreputable—a letter addressed by him to the Admiralty, containing a charge against Sir Hudson Lowe, which, if made at all, ought to have been made openly and substantiated by proof. This, therefore, must be set off against that appearance of credibility which is, as I think, distinguishable in O'Meara's book and in his conversation."

Lord Dudley's "impression" naturally counts for very little, but with regard to Sir George Cockburn two remarks may be made. First, Sir George Cockburn left St. Helena in June, 1816, which was considerably more than a year before the Governor had a breach with O'Meara, so he could know nothing personally of the merits of the case; and, secondly, Lord Bathurst wrote to Sir Hudson Lowe in November, 1818, that Sir G. Cockburn was the first person who, on reading the charges, declared that O'Meara ought to be instantly dismissed the service. Another statement (in the memoir of O'Meara) is: " On his [O'Meara's] return to England he was well received by the Lords of the Admiralty, and is said to have had the valuable post of surgeon to Greenwich Hospital offered to him." Yes, his " reception " consisted in his summary dis-

missal from his Majesty's service—if that is being
" well received "—and the insinuation about Greenwich
Hospital is simply untrue. Eighty years ago Mr. Finlaison—O'Meara's old correspondent—wrote in a letter
to the " Morning Chronicle ":[1]

" Mr. O'Meara having stated in the latter part of
his letter that I offered him the lucrative situation of
surgeon to Greenwich Hospital, I beg leave to state,
in the most distinct manner, that I never was authorized
to make any such proposition, and that, therefore, it is
but fair to presume that I never could have done so."

With regard to O'Meara's dismissal, the defence is
made that he could not have brought the charge at
the time, because Sir Hudson Lowe would have seen
it. But surely he could have written it direct to the
Ministry, just as he wrote to Mr. Finlaison without
the knowledge of the Governor, or again, as the
Secretary to the Admiralty reminded him, he could
have made the charge before the Admiral on the
station at St. Helena, who was independent of the
Governor. The defence made is simply childish. We
read again: " The accuracy of O'Meara's narrative is
emphatically endorsed by Count Las Cases." Very
probably it is. Las Cases, however, has quite enough
to do to look after his own character for "accuracy";
certainly he has not enough character for two.

Some of the most flagrant and obvious misstate-

[1] Of March 3rd, 1823.

ments of fact on the part of O'Meara are omitted; for instance, those contained in the entries of July 6th, 1816, and December 18th, 1817. The former entry is thoroughly exposed in the "Quarterly Review" article of October, 1822; the latter by Forsyth. Some of the language previously attributed to Lord Amherst, who called in at St. Helena on his return from China, is omitted, Lord Amherst having taken the trouble to disavow it expressly. With regard to omissions, the publishers state that some "purely repetitory passages have been omitted, also the story of the early days of Napoleon's butler, Cipriani." Under which heading do they class the omissions above specified? There is also an additional chapter professing to continue the narrative to the death of Napoleon. The writer faithfully imitates O'Meara in his regard for accuracy. For instance, he says that, in January, 1820, Napoleon "on several occasions breakfasted at the house of Sir Wm. Doveton on the other side of the island." Napoleon *once* only did so, and this was on October 4th, 1820.[1] Forsyth gives a minute description of it, as being a thing that only occurred *once*. Again, a description is given of a visit of Miss Susanna Johnson, "the young and pretty daughter of Lady Lowe," who "ventured to come alone to Longwood," and of her accidentally meeting the Emperor, who gave her a rose. For this

[1] On this occasion the worthy knight described Napoleon's appearance in a phrase more expressive than elegant: "He looked," he said, "as fat and as round as a China pig."

Montholon is quoted as authority; but the writer should have seen the absurdity of it, and Miss Lowe, the half-sister of Miss Johnson, writes: " A pure invention, such a thing was impossible."

Such then is the value of the evidence of the French and of O'Meara. They spoke of each other, it is true, in terms the reverse of flattering, but their object was the same—to further the political plans of Napoleon. The French attacked Sir Hudson Lowe on political grounds, O'Meara attacked him mainly for personal reasons. What evidence is there on the other side? To begin with, the charges are obviously over-stated. If true, they prove too much. If true, it is hardly conceivable that the admirals on the station in succession —viz., Sir Pulteney Malcolm, Admiral Plampin, and Admiral Lambert—would not have interfered. They, at any rate, cannot have been terrorized by Sir Hudson Lowe. Moreover, the character of a man is judged most correctly by those among whom he spends his life, for no man can be always acting. It is not denied that Sir Hudson Lowe was personally popular with the inhabitants of St. Helena. They voted him an address when leaving, which contained much more than conventional expressions of regret at his departure, and some years later (in 1828) when, returning from Ceylon, he called in at St. Helena, he was fêted enthusiastically by the people, who gratefully remembered the justice and kindliness of his rule.[1]

[1] See Appendix C.

I will now take the direct evidence in favour of Sir Hudson Lowe. First is that of Lieutenant-Colonel Basil Jackson, whom I have already had occasion to quote. He was a gentleman universally respected, and died so recently as 1889 at the patriarchal age of ninety-four. He first became known to Sir Hudson Lowe as serving on the Staff in the Netherlands in 1814 and 1815, and the impression which Sir Hudson Lowe made upon him on first acquaintance has already been given. The impression was mutually favourable, for, on being nominated Governor of St. Helena, Sir H. Lowe invited Lieutenant Jackson to accompany him. His duty was to keep Longwood House and its appurtenances in a habitable state, with strict orders to neglect nothing that could tend to promote the comfort of Napoleon and the persons of his suite. Probably Lieutenant Jackson was on more friendly terms with the French than any other Englishman, and so had exceptional opportunities of knowing their real sentiments. At a later period he was Lieutenant-Colonel in the Royal Staff Corps and Professor of Military Surveying at the East India College at Addiscombe. As Colonel Jackson uniformly speaks in favour of Sir Hudson Lowe, and as nothing whatever can be alleged against his character, an attempt has been made to detract from the weight of his testimony by the assertion that he was from early youth a *protégé* of Sir Hudson Lowe—an assertion which is perfectly untrue; and further, it has somehow got

abroad that Sir Hudson Lowe's second son, the late
Major-General Edward William De Lancy Lowe,
married a daughter of Colonel Jackson. This statement actually finds a place in the notice of Major-
General Lowe in the "Dictionary of National Biography," but it is a pure fabrication. As a matter of
fact Major-General Lowe never even met Miss Jackson.
As already noticed, directly after Sir Hudson Lowe's
death in January, 1844, Colonel Jackson wrote "A
Slight Tribute to the Memory of Sir Hudson Lowe,"
which appeared in the "United Service Magazine" for
March of that year. In 1877 he wrote "Notes and
Reminiscences of a Staff Officer, chiefly relating to
the Waterloo Campaign and to St. Helena matters
during the captivity of Napoleon," from which I have
quoted under the title of "Waterloo and St. Helena." [1]
As regards Sir H. Lowe, the tone of these reminiscences
is the same as that of the article written thirty-three
years earlier. I shall have to quote again from this
small volume. Meantime I give his description of the
Governor of St. Helena as he appeared in 1816: "He
stood 5 ft. 7 in., spare in make, having good features,
fair hair, and eyebrows overhanging his eyes; his look
denoted penetration and firmness, his manner rather
abrupt, his gait quick, his look and general demeanour
indicative of energy and decision. He was warm and
steady in his friendships, and popular both with the
inhabitants of the isle and the troops." Another

[1] On this book see above, pp. 9, 18.

witness, still more independent if possible than Colonel Basil Jackson, inasmuch as he never saw Sir Hudson Lowe till they met at St. Helena, is Mr. Walter Henry, Assistant-Surgeon of the 66th Regiment, who arrived in July, 1817, and remained till the end.[1] He was present at the *post mortem* examination of Napoleon and sailed to England with the French. I have already quoted from his book, " Events of a Military Life." He thus writes of the Governor:

" The Governor appeared to be much occupied with the cares and duties of his important and responsible office, and looked very like a person who would not let his prisoner escape if he could help it. From first impressions I entertained an opinion of him far from favourable; if therefore, notwithstanding this prepossession, my testimony should incline to the other side, I can truly state that the change took place from the weight of evidence, and in consequence of what came under my own observation in St. Helena. Since that time he has encountered a storm of obloquy and reproach enough to bow any person to the earth; yet I firmly believe that the talent he exerted in unravelling

[1] Lord Rosebery says of Mr. Henry: "Henry, throughout his two volumes, has a loyal and catholic devotion to all British governors, which does not exclude Lowe " ("Napoleon : the Last Phase," p. 67). This is, however, quite inconsistent with the passage I quote here from Henry's book, which shows that he only became Sir Hudson Lowe's friend after overcoming an unfavourable first impression.

the intricate plotting constantly going on at Long-wood, and the firmness in tearing it to pieces, with the unceasing vigilance he displayed in the discharge of his arduous and invidious duties, made him more enemies than any hastiness of temper, uncourteous-ness of demeanour, or severity in his measures, of which the world was taught to believe him guilty." [1]

Mr. Henry's evidence is entirely opposed to that of O'Meara, although he was on friendly terms with that individual until he lost his character. However, Henry's experiences at St. Helena, being merely an episode in his life and adventures, cannot from the nature of the case be as much known as they would have been if separately published. The evidence of these two gentlemen alone is sufficient to overthrow the gigantic fabric of fraud and misrepresentation which has for so many years done duty with the world, and more espe-cially with the British public, as the true history of Napoleon at St. Helena. I will, however, bring for-ward another witness. In 1876 the "St. James's Magazine" published a series of papers purporting to be written by one Stewart, a pretended confidential servant of Napoleon. "The man's statements are a tissue of ridiculous falsehoods," says Colonel Jackson. The late Admiral Rous, who was on the station at St. Helena during part of this period, and to whom reference is made in these papers, wrote to Sir

[1] Henry, ii. 9, 10.

Thomas Reade's son as follows, under date July 22nd, 1876:

" The account of Napoleon at St. Helena is a tissue of falsehoods. . . . I state, upon my honour, that I do not believe either Lowe or Reade [Sir Thomas Reade] was capable of performing any act derogatory to the character of a gentleman. To the best of my knowledge, all reports of ill-treatment to Napoleon were systematic falsehoods, fabricated with a view of keeping alive a sympathy in Europe to enable his friends to succeed in obtaining a more agreeable exile." [1]

We now come to the specific charges both against the British Government and against Sir Hudson Lowe, which I hope the reader may be disposed to regard *upon their merits*. But before coming to them it may be as well to say something (1) on the personal character of Sir H. Lowe, and (2) on certain special difficulties with which he had to contend.

(1) It may be at once allowed that Sir Hudson Lowe was not a perfect character. He had his failings, of course, like every one else. He felt keenly, perhaps too keenly, the responsibility of his position. The peace of the world, he was told, depended on the faithful execution of his trust. " There is only one thing now to look after, and that rests with you," was

[1] "Waterloo and St. Helena," pp. 183, 184.

the refrain continually dinned into his ears. He needed no arguments to convince him of the importance of his charge, and was sometimes pedantic in his adherence to the letter of his instructions. He was constantly referring the most trivial matters to the home authorities—even some matters of which he, being on the spot, was a far more competent judge than they could be.

In the most trivial incidents he traced some intrigue at Longwood. He was obsessed with the idea of Napoleon's escape as Mr. Dick was with King Charles's head. A good example of this is given by Montchenu (the French Commissioner) in the following account:

"Bonaparte, walking on Sunday morning with M. de Montholon, saw two cows approaching one of the gates of the inclosure. He went immediately to fetch his gun, loaded it with ball, then returned to put himself in ambush and aimed at the first cow, which he shot dead; he only wounded the second. The telegraph immediately gave information to the Governor, who hurried to the spot. As it is at least five miles from Plantation House to Longwood, the orderly officer had time to remark to Montholon that shooting with ball ought not to be allowed in this place because a sentinel or any one else might easily be killed. Montholon answered coldly that the Emperor had decided to kill anything that entered his garden. The Governor, after inspecting the carcass, returned home without any communication with the Longwood people. On his return I was at his house and he narrated the adventure to me and kept on repeating, 'With ball! with ball!' I asked him if the cows belonged to the Company. 'Yes,' he said.—'How did they enter?'—'A servant left the gate open.'—I began to laugh, saying, 'I don't believe in the open gate, for you know the strict principles of Bonaparte: he was in the garden, he saw the cows coming on, he opened the gate and made preparations for the expedition.' Suddenly the Governor's face was overcast, and after reflecting a long time, 'Do you think so?' he said.—'I don't doubt it. He knows that you often use these cows and he wished to deprive you of them, and perhaps to prove to you that he can still make himself feared.' This remark troubled his mind further."[1]

Whether this story is quite correctly reported or not, it is consistent enough with Sir Hudson Lowe's behaviour on other occasions. Even a slight sense of humour would have saved the situation. His correspondence shows an almost nervous anxiety to put things right. The determination of Napoleon to hold no personal intercourse with the Governor caused difficulties which might have been explained in a moment, but which, when set forth in the diplomatic style affected by Las Cases, Bertrand, or Montholon, assumed formidable proportions. Moreover, Sir Hud-

[1] "La Captivité de Ste.-Hélène," pp. 187-189.

son Lowe was not a good letter-writer. His sentences
are long and involved, and when he means to be
gracious—as he often does—there is an awkwardness
in expression which takes away the grace. The letter
he wrote about the gift of the chessmen, which is
quoted afterwards in another connexion, is a good
example.[1] It is a matter of everyday experience that,
where there is a difference of opinion, correspondence
only aggravates a dispute instead of allaying it, unless
there is very good will on both sides. Few can deny
themselves the temptation to achieve a verbal victory
over an opponent, which only produces further friction
and enlarges the ground of quarrel. And in this case
we know that the French attendants were delighted
to have the opportunity of exchanging letters with the
Governor. They used to show them about with appropriate comments, while Sir Hudson Lowe kept
matters secret. This secrecy was a mistake, for he had
nothing to be ashamed of. We have already noticed
it in the case of O'Meara's dismissal, and Lady Malcolm comments upon it after the last interview between
Napoleon and the Governor, pointing out how much
Sir Hudson Lowe's reputation suffered from his mistaken policy of enjoining secrecy, while Napoleon took
care to have his own version spread abroad quickly.[2]

Goethe says that he admires Englishmen because
they have the courage to be what they are, so

[1] See below, p. 219.
[2] See the passage quoted below, p. 187.

K

completely.[1] Sir Hudson Lowe was rather lacking in this kind of courage and completeness of character. If he had possessed a little more of the bluntness and completeness of Sir George Cockburn he could not, it is true, have satisfied Napoleon and his attendants (no one could have done that), but he would have spared himself an immense deal of worry, and would have appeared to more advantage in the eyes of the world. Again, he certainly showed a want of tact in some of his dealings with Napoleon. When the Emperor persistently refused to recognize the title of General Bonaparte, the only one by which the British Government would allow him to be addressed, it is hardly likely that he would have accepted an invitation to dinner from the Governor addressed to "General Bonaparte." This invitation to meet the Countess of Loudon, though made with the best intentions, was clearly a mistake, and it is no wonder that Napoleon regarded it as an insult. Near the close of his life Napoleon presented to the officers of the 20th Regiment, to which his then medical attendant, Dr. Arnott, belonged, Coxe's "Life of Marlborough," which had been given to him by the Hon. Robert Spencer. Unfortunately, the imperial title was written inside the books. On this account, though Sir Hudson Lowe

---

[1] See Eckermann's "Conversations with Goethe." The poet grants that they are sometimes complete fools It may be doubted whether this completeness of character is usually found in Englishmen at the present day.

did not forbid the acceptance of the volumes, he certainly discouraged it, and they were not accepted. Upon this incident one must agree with the remarks of Mr. Forsyth:

"I cannot help thinking that Napoleon's kindly-meant present might, under all the circumstances, have been accepted, notwithstanding the style of Emperor was inscribed in the volumes. He did not send them as coming from 'the Emperor,' nor write the objectionable title in them; nor was there much likelihood of a British regiment being seduced from its allegiance by adding to its library a few books, the gift of Napoleon. It does not appear that he ever heard of the fate of his present; but if he had there is no doubt that he would have felt what had happened as a deliberate insult."

Sir Hudson Lowe also showed a want of tact in endeavouring to settle questions of house accommodation and expenses with Napoleon direct, and thus gave a plausibility to the Emperor's taunt: "Il marchande ignominieusement notre existence."

There is too a consensus of opinion that the Governor's manner was abrupt and reserved, even in the judgement of those most favourably disposed towards him. His son says of him: "In speaking he was frequently embarrassed for words; and in society alternated very much between extreme taciturnity and

vehement animation of discourse. Even the greatest excitement, however, scarcely made his diction
fluent."[1]

Charity, we know on good authority, covers a multitude of sins, but a good manner covers many more.
"Manners," says Emerson, "are the happy ways of
doing things," and it must be allowed that Sir Hudson's way was often not happy. And his situation was
one in which it was of supreme importance not only
to act with kindness, consideration, and delicacy, but
also to seem to do so. He had to be not merely in
the right, but to be obviously in the right. His predecessor as Governor, Colonel Wilks, was much more
of a diplomatist, and kept on very good terms with
Napoleon during the six months they were together,
though no doubt the knowledge that his period of
office would so soon end, and the fact that he was not
charged with the care of Napoleon's person, much
helped the situation. Of the real goodness of heart of
Sir Hudson Lowe and his sincere efforts to do what he
could for the comfort of Napoleon and his suite there
is no doubt whatever, not only from his own declaration, but from the evidence of his conduct, as will be
seen later. Lady Malcolm's "Diary" tells us how frequently the Admiral impressed this upon Napoleon.
Even after the Emperor had refused to hold personal
intercourse with the Governor, the latter still con-

[1] "United Service Magazine," June, 1844, p. 295. But surely
the tendency of excitement is to make the diction less fluent.

tinued to show him every attention and to gratify all his desires so far as was consistent with his own duty.[1]

(2) Besides the difficulties inseparable from his position, Sir Hudson Lowe had others of an external nature. These were the presence of three foreign Commissioners and the conduct of the home Government towards himself. These subjects are so important that a separate chapter must be devoted to them.

[1] See the passage from Henry quoted p. 216 below.

CHAPTER VII

LOWE'S DIFFICULTIES

Convention of August 2nd, 1815.—The foreign Commissioners.
—Conduct of the British Government towards Sir Hudson
Lowe.

UNDER a convention dated the 2nd of August,
1815, and made between Great Britain, Austria,
Russia, and Prussia, it was declared: "(1) Napoleon
Bonaparte is considered by the Powers . . . as their
prisoner. (2) His custody is especially entrusted to the
British Government. . . . (3) The Courts of Austria,
Russia, and Prussia are to appoint Commissioners to
proceed to and abide at the place which the Government of his Britannic Majesty shall have assigned for
the residence of Napoleon Bonaparte, and who, without
being responsible for his custody, will assure themselves
of his presence." The King of France was also invited
to send a Commissioner.[1] In Count Balmain's instructions the object of the convention is stated to be "to
give a European character to the affair, and to make
it clear that Bonaparte is the prisoner of Europe."[2]

[1] The text of this convention is given in Forsyth, i. 435.
[2] See Balmain's instructions given in Schlitter's edition of
Stürmer's "Reports," p. 159.

It would therefore operate as a guard against any attempt to recall Napoleon from exile in the event of a change of Government in Great Britain. From every other aspect the appointment of these Commissioners was not merely useless, but a great source of anxiety and annoyance to the Governor. The editor of Montchenu's reports says: " It will be seen that the mission of the Commissioners was almost useless; it was, besides, deadly dull for them, expensive for the Courts which sent them, and added nothing to the safe guardianship of the Emperor."[1] Austria sent out Baron Stürmer, Russia Count Balmain, and France the Marquis de Montchenu. Prussia, probably from economical motives, did not avail herself of her power under the convention. The three Commissioners arrived with Admiral Malcolm June 17th, 1816. As Great Britain had undertaken the duty of guarding Napoleon and would naturally not be interfered with, they had nothing in the world to do except to pass their time, which they did, partly by enjoying the Governor's hospitality, and partly—at least in the case of two of them—by engaging in intrigues against his authority with the French. They transmitted reports to their respective Governments, but as Napoleon would not receive them in their official capacity, and as Sir Hudson Lowe would not allow them to be presented as private individuals, they had not much of importance to transmit. Lord Bathurst urged Sir Hudson

[1] G. Firmin-Didot's " Captivité de Sainte-Hélène," p. 19.

Lowe to encourage the Commissioners "to amuse themselves by going to the Cape by way of change of scene"; and Napoleon himself exclaimed: "What folly it is to send those Commissioners out here without charge or responsibility! They will have nothing to do but to walk about the streets and creep up the rocks."[1]

All three Commissioners have left copious accounts of themselves and their mission. The official despatches of the Austrian and the Russian Commissioners have been published, while M. Georges Firmin-Didot has written "La Captivité de Sainte-Hélène" after the reports of the French Commissioner. These documents are well worth reading on their own account, and as regards the character of Sir Hudson Lowe generally they furnish important evidence. It has been represented that the Commissioners were impartial witnesses, and that their evidence is uniformly unfavourable to the Governor.[2] This view, however, cannot be accepted. In the case of Stürmer and of Montchenu their instructions—or, at least, their interpretation of them—precluded impartiality by placing them in antagonism to the Governor, nor were any of the three uniformly unfavourable to him. But we might go further and say that even if they had been more impartial and more unfavourable than

[1] Forsyth, i. 190, 191.

[2] See Lord Rosebery's chapter on the Commissioners, which is one of the best in his book.

they are, the charges from which Sir Hudson Lowe is being here defended relate, not to his behaviour towards them, but to his behaviour towards Napoleon. Not wishing, however, to narrow the issue in this way, we proceed to consider what they have written. They are much more credible witnesses than the French, inasmuch as they did not deliberately misrepresent facts according to a concerted "plan of campaign." They are, at any rate, more or less honest witnesses. The instructions of the Austrian and the French Commissioners were practically identical. The chief points were: (1) to assure themselves "by their own eyes" of the presence of Napoleon on the island; (2) to draw up a *procès-verbal* to be signed by all the Commissioners and countersigned by the Governor, and to transmit a copy of this *procès-verbal* to their respective Courts every month; (3) to give immediate information to the Governor of any attempt to escape, etc., of which knowledge or rumour might come to them; (4) to have no relations whatever with Bonaparte or with the persons of his suite, and to inform the Governor of attempts made by others to establish such relations; (5) to act in common with the Commissioners of the other Courts. The instructions of Count Balmain from the Russian Court were not so strict. Only the following extract need be given:

"Your part will be purely passive; you will observe everything and give an account of everything. In your relations with the English authorities you will show the conciliatory spirit suitable to the bonds of alliance and friendship which unite the two Courts. In your relations with Bonaparte you will observe the respect and the moderation that so delicate a situation requires *et les égards personnels qu'on lui doit.* You will neither avoid nor seek opportunities for seeing him, and in this respect you will conform strictly to the rules that may be established by the Governor."[1]

There is nothing here about seeing Napoleon " with your own eyes " or drawing up a *procès-verbal.* How then could the Commissioners act in unison? On arrival, the first thing done by Stürmer and Montchenu was to draw up a joint note requesting the Governor to procure for them " the earliest opportunity of seeing Napoleon Bonaparte."[2] Count Balmain naturally held aloof from this request. Sir Hudson Lowe had no knowledge of the special instructions of the Commissioners. He had merely been informed generally by Lord Bathurst that they were to reside in St. Helena in order that the Powers might receive direct reports of the security of Bonaparte's person, and that they were to be simply correspondents of their re-

---

[1] See Montchenu's and Balmain's instructions set out in Stürmer, pp. 156-159. The words in italics in Balmain's instructions were underlined by the Emperor Alexander, and Napoleon, when he was aware of them, conveyed his thanks to the Russian Emperor through Count Balmain.

[2] The note is given in Stürmer, p. 155.

spective Courts.[1] Being thus taken by surprise, the
Governor was not prepared to act in any high-handed
way to gratify them at the cost of Napoleon's comfort.
It is no wonder that he wrote to Lord Bathurst:
" The whole appear to have come out with the impression that not only there could be no difficulty in
seeing Bonaparte, but that they could at once be admitted to terms of habitual and free intercourse with
him."[2] Montchenu in particular, prompted by his
foolish vanity, brought matters to an issue at once by
demanding a guard of soldiers to force his way into
the Emperor's presence! In face of the Commissioners' instructions Sir Hudson Lowe did not give a
formal refusal to this modest demand, but, short of
that, opposed it with all his influence, and it was
withdrawn.

When Napoleon had seen a copy of the convention
of the 2nd of August (which could not be found for
three weeks, and then in an old newspaper), he naturally declined to see the Commissioners in their official
capacity, as that would be considered an acknowledgement that he was a prisoner *de iure* as well as *de facto*,
but he often expressed his willingness to see them as
individuals. Here, however, the Governor stepped in,
and, although he was personally willing that a private
visit should be paid, he was really waiting for instructions from home on this point. The instructions,

---

[1] Part of Sir Hudson Lowe's instructions: see Forsyth, i. 438.
[2] Given in Forsyth, i. 197.

when they arrived, bade him discourage such visits, and they were not paid, and as a fact none of the Commissioners ever saw Napoleon in life; one only—Montchenu—saw him dead. "When we asked," writes Stürmer, " M. de Montchenu and myself, to see Bonaparte as Commissioners, the Governor said to Count Balmain, ' These gentlemen wish me to show him to them like a chained bear.' When Count Balmain in his turn desired to see Bonaparte as a private individual, the Governor said to me, ' How can Count Balmain think of seeing him except as Commissioner!'"[1]

There was also another question with the Commissioners which caused a difficulty. Were they to be regarded as coming under the provisions of the Act of Parliament of April 11th, 1816 (56 Geo. III. c. 22), which prescribed the most severe punishment for all persons "being a subject or subjects of or owing allegiance to his Majesty" who should in any way aid or abet an attempt to escape on the part of Napoleon? In other words, were they to be considered for this purpose as "owing allegiance" to the King? They vehemently protested that they were not, but opinions were divided on the point. At last, in July, 1817, instructions arrived from England that the Commissioners were not personally liable to the pains and penalties of the Act, but that their servants were to be so considered. We cannot be surprised

[1] Stürmer, p. 105.

that an attitude of perfect impartiality towards the Governor was a difficult one for the Commissioners to maintain.

Baron Stürmer soon had troubles of his own. He had brought out in his suite a botanist named Welle, who, it turned out, was charged with the conveyance to Napoleon of a lock of his son's hair and with a letter to General Gourgaud, both of which he secretly delivered. As rumours of this matter reached the Governor's ears, and as such secret delivery was forbidden by the regulations, he naturally applied to Baron Stürmer. The latter at first denied the facts, and so aroused the Governor's suspicions, but the event proved that the Governor was right. As Sir Hudson said, reasonably enough, he did not object to Napoleon's having a lock of his son's hair, but to the clandestine way in which the gift was conveyed. In this affair Stürmer was no doubt innocent, but he might have made himself better informed.[1] At a later time he had unauthorized communications with Napoleon's suite, and was rebuked in despatches from the Austrian Court. In August, 1818, he was removed to another post in Brazil with all outward show of honour, but really because of his want of accommodation with the Governor. In so difficult a situation it is impossible to assign much blame to either side ; but we cannot wonder that the Austrian Commissioner

[1] A great deal of Stürmer's reports is taken up with the Welle incident.

regarded Sir Hudson Lowe with no very friendly feelings. Stürmer recounts some amusing interviews with Lowe. What he chiefly disliked in the Governor was his excessive reserve. He could get nothing out of him. When Stürmer asked what information he could give his Court, "the Governor replied that he was naturally uncommunicative, but that as he made it his duty to inform his Government of everything even to the minutest details, the latter would communicate to our Courts, if it thought proper, anything that might interest them."[1] Sir Hudson Lowe felt, no doubt, that in logical fence he was no match for Stürmer, who had had a diplomatic training, and wisely held his tongue—on one occasion, we read, at an interview with Stürmer he kept silence for twenty minutes. Stürmer was not over-scrupulous. He applied to his Government to know what he was to do in case Napoleon should send for him. "Ought I," he asks, "if the Governor opposes it, to go there without his consent? Ought I to give him an account of what Bonaparte may say to me, or shall I limit myself *à lui faire une fausse confidence*? Finally, ought I to charge myself, or not, with any papers they may wish to entrust to me?"[2] On the other hand he testifies to the Governor's considerate behaviour towards Napoleon : "General Lowe treats him with all possible respect,

[1] Stürmer, p. 50. The Governor said just the same to Montchenu (see Balmain, p. 619).

[2] Stürmer, p. 103.

and even in some degree lends himself to his mania
of playing the Emperor. In spite of that, the latter
does not like him, and has only seen him two or three
times."[1]

Count Balmain, the Russian Commissioner, was the
most reasonable of the three, and did the best service
to his Government. His instructions, as we have seen,
did not place him at variance with Sir Hudson Lowe.
His despatches were first published in the Russian
archives, but are better known by their publication in
the "Revue Bleue" of May and June, 1897.[2] They are
interesting as recording the observation of an acute
and self-contained man of the world. He was originally appointed for three years, but stayed a year
longer at the request of his Court, by whom his conduct was always approved. A short time before his
departure, which was in May, 1820, he married Miss
Charlotte Johnson, the elder of Lady Lowe's two
daughters by her first husband. Lord Rosebery says,
on the authority of the anonymous editor in the
" Revue Bleue," " she seems afterwards to have amused
the Court of St. Petersburg by her eccentricities and
her accent."[3] However that may be, the Emperor
Alexander in 1823 introduced himself to the Countess
Balmain at Verona, and speaking to her of Sir Hudson

[1] Stürmer, p. 41.

[2] An English version was published lately in the "Daily
Mail," in September and October, 1902.

[3] Rosebery, p. 143; Balmain, p. 578.

Lowe, said: " Je l'estime beaucoup. Je l'ai connu dans des temps critiques."[1] Lord Rosebery states that Count Balmain's courtship " hampered him in the expression of his opinions," but it is difficult to find any trace of this, nor should we readily believe it. Experience shows, on the contrary, that connexions by marriage —even prospective connexions—are usually the most candid of critics. And here the criticism would not even be seen by the intended stepfather-in-law. The general impression derived from a perusal of Count Balmain's despatches is that he, like Admiral Malcolm, found Sir Hudson Lowe a difficult person to get on with, and in order to remain on good terms with him he was obliged to make certain sacrifices to the Governor's scruples. On his part Sir Hudson evidently had a regard for Balmain, and consulted him as a friend on occasion. But there is in these despatches no serious charge made against Lowe. He speaks of the pains the Governor took to please Napoleon, but without success, in precisely the same terms as Stür- mer does, whose words have been already quoted.[2] His own opinion of Sir Hudson Lowe quite agrees with what we know from other sources. " Sir Hudson Lowe," he says, " is certainly a worthy man, a man of honour and uprightness, besides being well educated.

[1] From a letter in the possession of Miss Lowe.

[2] As the language is identical, it is evident that Stürmer copied from Balmain, whose report is the earlier. Stürmer's reports, as well as Balmain's, were written in French.

But in business he is crushed by his weight of responsibility, he takes alarm at the least thing, and worries his brain over the merest trifles." [1] Balmain made a serious attempt to reconcile Lowe and the French attendants of Napoleon. He said to Gourgaud: "Make peace with him. He is an honest man. He bears no malice. He desires to be on good terms with you." [2] Gourgaud, however, naturally declined ; for where would they be without their grievances ? No doubt the excessive responsibility, to use a common phrase, got on the Governor's nerves, just as Napoleon had got on the nerves of the European Governments, and Lowe said and did many things which a less conscientious and less sensitive man would not have said and done.

The French Commissioner, the Marquis de Montchenu, appears to have been a compound of absurdity and vanity. In the book founded on his reports he is apologized for by his editor, [3] and even by his own secretary, M. de Gors, who accompanied him to St. Helena. "He has chattered too much," he says, "always blamed what *he* did not do, and never acted when it was time." [4] Napoleon, who had known him many years before, spoke of Montchenu with the greatest contempt as "one of those men who support the old prejudice that Frenchmen are nothing but

---

[1] Balmain, p. 620.   [2] *Ibid.*, p. 648.
[3] "La Captivité de Ste.-Hélène," by Georges Firmin-Didot.
[4] *Ibid.*, p. 30.

L

mountebanks."[1] Stürmer says that he had little education and was absolutely devoid of tact. As might be expected, Montchenu is not backward in returning these compliments. On the departure of Count Balmain he wrote to his Government: "There is no need to depict to you all his extravagances, his folly, the weakness and absurdity of his character. I only wish to prove to you how difficult he and M. de Stürmer have made my position."[2] The value of the opinion of Montchenu, however, is so absolutely *nil* that his abuse can hardly be regarded as a compliment—it is merely of no account. And yet it is to a large extent by quotations from his reports that the collective unfavourable judgement of the Commissioners upon Sir Hudson Lowe is founded!

Colonel Jackson says Montchenu was fond of going out to whist parties, but seldom invited others to his own house. From this circumstance he acquired the sobriquet of "le Marquis de Monter-chez-nous."[3] Mr. Henry gives an amusing account of how he attended the Marquis during an illness, for which he thought he had a right to expect some pecuniary fee. But the excellent Marquis gave him something much more valuable in the shape of a note—of thanks, which is printed in full as a model for future Commissioners who may wish to pay their doctors economically and

---

[1] "La Captivité de Ste.-Hélène," p. 5; Stürmer, p. 77.
[2] "La Captivité de Ste.-Hélène," p. 190.
[3] "Waterloo and St. Helena," p. 139.

yet handsomely. "Who," he adds, "would exchange such a letter for a gold snuff-box? I am quite certain that I never shall." Incidentally Mr. Henry here testifies to the Governor's kindness of heart. The Marquis was recommended change of air. "As soon as Sir Hudson Lowe heard this he invited him to Plantation House; and I rode there to see him two or three times a week until his health became perfectly re-established."

It was Montchenu, it will be remembered, who spoilt the Commissioners' chances of seeing Napoleon by his proposal to have recourse to violence. He was the only one of the three who remained to the end, and when it had become perfectly clear that the Commissioners had nothing to do he was allowed to represent Austria and Russia as well as France. This empty honour inflated him still more, and at length he proclaimed to the Governor his intention of visiting the French at Longwood: "If," he declared, "you cause the gate to be closed by a sentinel, you know that I do not understand English, and should not comprehend what he says; but I will pass on, even if he were to fire at me a shot which would soon re-echo through the whole of Europe."[1] The Governor, however, would not let him go, and he did not feel bold enough to face the fire of the sentinel.

The presence of the Commissioners was, then, a great embarrassment to Sir Hudson Lowe in the discharge

[1] Forsyth, iii. 240.

of his duty; but the worst thing of all, and that which put so much power into the hands of O'Meara, was the conduct of the British Government, which, viewed in itself, was utterly undignified; viewed from Sir Hudson Lowe's standpoint, was unfair and treacherous. As before stated, O'Meara carried on a regular correspondence with Mr. Finlaison of the Admiralty, and was encouraged by Cabinet Ministers to write copious letters of gossip about Napoleon for the amusement of themselves and the Prince Regent! It is true Sir Hudson was informed of this after it had gone on for a long time, but it utterly stultified the express instructions of the Government as to correspondence. Thus O'Meara was emboldened to defy the authority of Sir Hudson Lowe, and if it had not been for his own infatuation he might have done so to the end. Mr. Henry's remarks on this are worth quoting. He says:

" I have been informed since, on authority which I cannot doubt, that Mr. O'Meara had a friend in London, the private secretary of Lord M[elvi]lle, who found it convenient to have a correspondent in St. Helena, then a highly interesting spot, who should give him all the gossip of the island for the First Lord of the Admiralty, to be sported in a higher circle afterwards for the Prince Regent's amusement. The patronage of Lord M. was thus secured; and Mr. O'Meara, confident on this backing, stood out stiffly against Sir

Hudson Lowe. The latter was quite ignorant of this intrigue against the proper exercise of his authority; and when he discovered it afterwards he found it was a delicate matter to meddle with, involving the conduct of a Cabinet Minister, and affecting, possibly, the harmony of the Ministry. Even after the development of the vile poisoning charge against the Governor, the influence of the First Lord was exerted to screen O'Meara, but in vain; for Lord Liverpool exclaimed, as in another well-known instance of a very different description, ' It is too bad! ' " [1]

.Thus, while one Cabinet Minister was writing to Sir Hudson Lowe commending him for his vigilance, and urging particular care to prevent clandestine correspondence, another Cabinet Minister was doing all he could to undermine the Governor's authority by encouraging a clandestine correspondence! Mr. Forsyth has not made enough of this. What Governor ever before had at the same time to fight against open foes and treacherous friends? Fortunately for others, especially for the British Government, O'Meara was the sort of man who, if given enough rope, would be sure to hang himself; and so it proved. The Government did not, therefore, reap the full consequences of their own folly. It is certainly no thanks to *them* that Napoleon did not effect his escape.

Sir Hudson Lowe was too loyal to make any formal

[1] Henry, ii. 43.

complaint, but a consciousness of the unfair position in which he was placed is evident in a memorial to Lord Liverpool which he drew up in 1824. It is indeed incredible, as Sir Hudson Lowe there remarks, that the members of the Government who enjoyed O'Meara's gossip intended in the first instance that he should be the medium of communication to them of important state information. Yet O'Meara saw his advantage and immediately seized it. He delivered up to Sir Hudson Lowe a letter written by Count Montholon (the celebrated "Remonstrance") which had been left in his room for the purpose of being sent home to be published in the "Morning Chronicle," and of which he said to the Governor that he intended to make no other use than to take extracts from it for a friend in the Admiralty. He also exhibited a letter marked "secret and confidential," encouraging his correspondence, but not communications of this kind. The Governor then cautioned him upon his correspondence with any individual upon matters of so delicate a nature, and added that the Governor himself was the proper channel for communications to his Majesty's Ministers. The merit would not be the less O'Meara's, as any information he might give would be conveyed in his own name. In spite of this, however, O'Meara resolved on a continuance of his communications, and, in order to obtain a guarantee for them, boldly made known the injunctions that had been laid upon him by Sir Hudson Lowe, and his arguments for disobeying them, and actually transmitted at the same time a copy of the very letter he had delivered up! Two months later he sent a still fuller communication, repeated the Governor's injunctions, and resolved to bring the question to an issue, " as to the approbation or otherwise that might be bestowed upon the continuance of his opposition in so important a point to the officer under whose authority he was placed." The replies to that letter were decisive as to the nature of Sir Hudson Lowe's future relations, not only with O'Meara himself, but with Napoleon (who had the wires thus placed in his own hands), with his followers, with the foreign Commissioners, to whom their purport must have been secretly communicated, and in short with all descriptions of persons whom there was any object in letting into the secret.

"Words cannot convey," continues the Governor, " in more precise terms the approbation bestowed on the conduct of the person written to. It is unnecessary to say that this unfortunate proceeding rendered tenfold more difficult the execution of Sir Hudson Lowe's duties at St. Helena, and made it almost impossible for him to come to any right understanding with the persons under his charge—secretly stripped him of one of the chief attributes of his authority, while leaving him still the responsible person for the mischief which might spring from such interference with it."

At a later period, when the British Government

abandoned Sir Hudson Lowe's reputation to the ill-instructed indignation of the public, some Ministers must have been more ready to sacrifice him from their own consciousness of the injury they had done him while he was at St. Helena.

CHAPTER VIII

GOVERNMENT ORDERS

Cause of Napoleon's death.—Instructions to Admiral Cockburn.
—Instructions to Sir Hudson Lowe.

IN considering the charges against Sir Hudson
Lowe, a clear distinction must be drawn between
the acts of the British Government, in carrying out
which the Governor was acting officially, and the personal acts of Sir Hudson Lowe.

The climate of St. Helena has already been discussed.[1] As to the death of Napoleon, all the doctors
who attended the *post mortem* examination certified
that the disease of which the Emperor died was cancer of the stomach—a disease which, I need hardly
say, is unaffected by climate. O'Meara was absolutely
wrong in his diagnosis of "chronic hepatitis," and it is
a very remarkable fact *that it was owing to the good
condition of the liver that life was preserved so long.*
"The liver acted as a kind of cork or stopper to
the opening in the coat of the stomach formed by
the ulcer, and prevented the escape of the contents

[1] See above, pp. 81-83.

of the stomach, which must have caused immediate death." [1]

If Napoleon was to be detained at St. Helena certain measures had to be taken to prevent his escape, and also to prevent communications with adherents in Europe or elsewhere, who might form conspiracies and raise revolutions. The instructions issued to Sir Hudson Lowe were included by reference in those issued to Admiral Cockburn. The chief points in the latter, dated July 30th, 1815, so far as they relate to the detention at St. Helena, and after a statement that every indulgence was to be allowed General Bonaparte consistent with the security of his person, were the following:

"(11) The General must be always attended by an officer appointed by the Admiral or Governor, as the case may be.[2] If the General be permitted to move beyond the boundaries where the sentries are placed, the officer should be attended by one orderly at least.

"(12) . . . They who accompany him to St. Helena

---

[1] Forsyth, iii. 293, and Dr. Shortt's evidence there quoted; also Montholon's letter to his wife already given (p. 88).

[2] From October, 1815, to April, 1816, when Sir Hudson Lowe arrived, the care of Napoleon was entrusted to Admiral Cockburn, while Colonel Wilks remained Governor of the island. Sir Hudson Lowe combined the functions of both. The instruction that Napoleon should be "always attended by an officer" was never carried out either by Cockburn or Lowe. He was only attended by an officer when he went outside the boundaries.

. . . are to reside with him; and it is left to the discretion of the Admiral in the first instance, and to the new Governor afterwards, to establish such regulations with respect to them at other times [*i.e.*, other than the arrival of ships] as may appear expedient.

"(15) All letters addressed to him, or his attendants, must be first delivered to the Admiral, or to the Governor, as the case may be, who will read them before they are delivered to the persons to whom they are addressed. All letters written by the General or his attendants must be subject to the same regulation.

"(16) No letter which has not been transmitted to St. Helena by the Secretary of State should be delivered to the General, or to those who accompany him, if it be written by any person not resident in the island; and all their letters addressed to persons not resident in the island must be sent under cover to the Secretary of State.

"(17) The General must be given clearly to understand that the Governor and Admiral are strictly instructed to forward to his Majesty's Government any wish or representation which he may think proper to make to the British Government; and in that particular they are not at liberty to exercise any discretion; but the paper on which such application or representation may be written must be left open for their joint inspection, in order that in transmitting it they may be enabled to accompany it with such observations as they may think expedient.

"(24) An order for preventing, after due notice, foreign ships, and ships belonging to the private trade, from resorting to St. Helena, will be forthwith given."

The instructions of the British Government to Sir Hudson Lowe are contained in a despatch of September 12th, 1815, from Lord Bathurst, Secretary of State for War and the Colonies, in which, after a reference to an inclosed copy of the Memorandum to Admiral Cockburn for his guidance, it is written:

"(4) I have little to add to the directions which are contained in this Memorandum; and you will observe them as the general principles by which your conduct is to be regulated. Many things, however, must be determined by local circumstances; and the experience which I have already had of your judgement and discretion makes me repose this most important trust, without apprehension, in your hands. You will observe that the desire of his Majesty's Government is to allow every indulgence to General Bonaparte which may be compatible with the entire security of his person: that he should not by any means escape, or hold communication with any person whatever (excepting through your agency), must be your unremitted care; and these points being made sure, every resource and amusement which may serve to reconcile Bonaparte to his confinement may be permitted."

Lord Bathurst also tells Sir Hudson Lowe of the arrival of the foreign Commissioners. The Governor considered that his instructions differed from those issued to Cockburn only in the point that Napoleon was not to communicate with any person whatever except through his agency, but this was probably not an intentional addition—certainly Cockburn had acted up to it. After studying his instructions Sir Hudson Lowe wrote to Sir Henry Bunbury asking the precise nature and quality of Napoleon's situation. Was he to be considered as a prisoner of war, or as a state prisoner, or otherwise? He also suggested that an Act should be passed declaring it felony to aid or abet Napoleon's escape, adding:

" I should much prefer a definite authority on all points over that of being permitted to exercise any kind of arbitrary jurisdiction whatever, particularly such as is usually practised under the ill-defined rules of martial law. . . . In submitting any measures that may appear to bear the character of extraordinary rigour, I beg at the same time to express that *harshness* is by no means the principle on which I should propose to regulate my proceedings."[1]

The answer was that Sir Hudson Lowe was to treat Napoleon as a prisoner of war until further orders, and on the 11th of April, 1816, an Act was passed (55

[1] Forsyth, i. 443-445.

Geo. III. c. 22) in the sense which Sir Hudson Lowe desired, and the next day a warrant was issued to him under the Act.

It will be observed that three of the most important regulations, and those which produced the greatest irritation in Napoleon and his attendants, are not specifically mentioned in these official documents. I refer to the refusal to acknowledge the title of Emperor and the resulting obligation on the part of the Governor to allow no presents bearing the imperial insignia to reach Napoleon, the order that Napoleon should be seen twice every twenty-four hours by an officer, and the refusal to grant Plantation House (the Governor's residence) for the use of Napoleon. All three regulations, however, were in reality part of the Government instructions, as will be seen, and there was no liberty to change them. Sir Hudson Lowe considered the two leading points of his instructions to be personal security and the prevention of unauthorized communication. It is generally represented that the restrictions imposed were unnecessarily severe, and that they were rendered much more intolerable by the harshness and brutality of the Governor in carrying them out. An examination will show that as regards the Governor the precise opposite was the case. The severity of the restrictions, such as it was, was much mitigated by the kindness and consideration of Sir Hudson Lowe, and the nearest approach to a rebuke that he ever received from the Government was owing to his not insisting sufficiently upon their instructions being obeyed. In October, 1820, H.M.S. *Owen Glendower*, commanded by the Hon. Robert Spencer, arrived at St. Helena. Captain Spencer arrived prepossessed in Napoleon's favour and believing that he was harshly treated, but before quitting the island he quite changed his opinion and said to the Governor that "if the precautions erred in any way, it was more on the side of indulgence than unnecessary restraint."

As Napoleon did not consider that the British Government had any right to confine him at all, it is not to be wondered at that he complained of each and every of the restrictions. Many have thought that it would have been more dignified on his part and more consonant with the position of one who had at one time enjoyed almost unlimited power, to have received the blows of fate with silence if not with equanimity, and sometimes he would have the world believe that such indeed was his attitude, as Montholon writes in the postscript to his well-known protest to the Governor of the 23rd of August, 1816 :

" Are your Ministers not aware that the sight of a great man struggling with adversity is the most sublime of spectacles? Can they be ignorant that Napoleon at St. Helena, in the midst of persecutions of every kind, to which he opposes only the most perfect serenity, is greater, more sacred, more venerated, than when he sat on the loftiest throne of the world, where he was so long the arbitrator of kings? Those who, in such circumstances, are wanting towards Napoleon, only degrade themselves and the nation they represent." [1]

But the choice spirits to whom such an attitude appeals are few in number, and have little influence on the course of events. Such is not usually the attitude of fallen heroes, and it was not that of Napoleon, who well knew that in order to excite the sympathy of the multitude he must make the voice of his complaints heard through Europe. The Act of Parliament authorizing the detention of Napoleon said that he should be " treated and dealt with as a prisoner of war." As the term " prisoner of war " connoted a certain line of treatment, Napoleon had a fair opportunity of complaining that he was not treated as a " prisoner of war " should be treated. " No instance," he says, " will be cited in the history of Great Britain or of France in which prisoners of war were sent away to be in a state of detention in another hemisphere, and on an isolated rock in the midst of the seas "; and again: " Prisoners of war, when they fall into the power of

---

[1] Firmin-Didot, p. 84 ; Forsyth, i. 266. That Napoleon was not unwilling to be regarded as a type of glorified humanity is clear from his extraordinary remark to Lady Malcolm—if it is to be taken seriously: " I have worn the imperial crown of France, the iron crown of Italy; England has now given me a greater and more glorious than either of them, for it is that worn by the Saviour of the world—a crown of thorns " (Lady Malcolm's " Diary," p. 159).

the enemy, are legitimated by the title which they bore at home."[1] All this may be true enough, and the only answer is the sufficient one that Napoleon was in fact something different from a "prisoner of war." His complaint that the Act of Parliament was an act of proscription is true. His detention was justified, and was only justifiable, on the ground that it was "necessary for the preservation of the tranquillity of Europe, and for the general safety," as the preamble of the Act states—in itself an extraordinary tribute to the power of one man. No question of legality can be raised. The detention of Napoleon must be justified by the same reasoning as justified the deposition of Charles I. It was a struggle to the death between two parties, where the winner is justified by his victory. Another complaint of Napoleon against the restrictions appears to us merely childish. It was that Napoleon claimed the strict execution of the Act of Parliament of April 11th, 1816, which, he contended, "limited the right of imposing restrictions to the Government, and did not give it to any individual."[1] This is simply a misapplication of the legal motto, *delegatus non potest delegare*, to which the answer is that a Government is not *delegatus*.

[1] From the observations dictated by Napoleon on Lord Bathurst's speech, Forsyth, ii. 349.

[2] *Ibid.*, ii. 212.

CHAPTER IX

CASE AGAINST GOVERNMENT

(1) Question of title.—(2) Correspondence.—(3) Personal
inspection.—(4) Residence.—(5) Limits.

THE principal specific instructions of the Government were the following :

(1) *That Napoleon was not to be allowed the title of
Emperor, but was always to be styled General Bonaparte.*
Though this is not contained in the instructions, it
may be remarked that the name Napoleon Bonaparte
(or General Bonaparte) was constantly used by the
British Government since the surrender at Rochefort.
There was no question of the title of Emperor. He is
called Napoleon Bonaparte in the Declaration at the
Vienna Congress of the 13th of March, 1815, when
the escape from Elba was known, also in the Convention of the 2nd of August, 1815 ; and the Act of 11th
April, 1816 (55 Geo. III. c. 22), is intituled " An Act
for the more effectually detaining in custody Napoleon
Buonaparte." This restriction was from first to last a
source of endless discomfort and difficulty. Certainly
the British Government were technically justified in
their refusal to allow the title of Emperor to one whom

they had not recognized as such in the height of his prosperity, and Sir Walter Scott strenuously defends them; but it is just because they had refused the title to the Emperor *then* that they could afford to be generous *now*. I am, therefore, of the opinion of Henry, Forsyth, and Lord Rosebery, that it is a point which might have been conceded without loss of dignity. Mr. Forsyth observes:

" It seemed puerile in us to ignore a title by which he will be known in history as certainly as Augustus or Charlemagne. It cannot be urged that to recognize Napoleon as Emperor would have been to abandon the cause of the Bourbons, for we had previously concluded the treaty of Amiens with him as the *de facto* ruler of France; and we had no right to impose either a king or a form of government upon that country." [1]

However this may be, all the odium of insisting upon this point fell upon Sir Hudson Lowe, who had no choice in the matter. We cannot be surprised that Napoleon himself and his attendants always insisted upon the title of " Emperor," and Sir Hudson Lowe was often obliged to return letters and other documents to them in consequence. At the same time he did this as a matter of form, and after having taken copies of the contents, with a view to considering any complaints that might be therein contained. Admiral Malcolm

[1] Forsyth, i. 42.

tells us that the Governor, with a view of being civil, avoided naming him as much as possible,[1] and after a time he used to speak of the ex-Emperor to the French attendants as Napoleon Bonaparte, a name which offended them less than General Bonaparte.[2] However, the Governor's refusal to allow the simple " Napoleon " to be written on the coffin showed a pedantic adherence to instructions which cannot be commended. To quarrel over a name at such a moment was ungracious.

Soon after the arrival of Sir Hudson Lowe, all Napoleon's suite and servants had to sign a declaration of submission to the terms on which they were to be allowed to remain on the island, and the Governor allowed them to refer to Napoleon as "the Emperor." In consequence of this all the declarations were sent back by Government and had to be signed over again without any mention of the obnoxious title. There was then some theatrical display, Napoleon's suite at first declaring that they would rather be sent away than submit to such a degradation, as they professed to consider it. However, when they found that Sir Hudson Lowe was not to be trifled with on this point they gave in, General Gourgaud setting the example, much, it appeared, to the relief of Napoleon.[3]

(2) *That no letters or packets were to be sent or received by the French unless they were first seen by the Governor.* This restriction was most vexatious, and,

---

[1] Lady Malcolm's "Diary," p. 14.
[2] See Forsyth, ii. 211. [3] *Ibid.*, i. 327.

after all, useless. Sir Walter Scott observes most truly
that when this restriction was placed upon *all* communications, any person would feel a certain amount
of sympathy, and be disposed to aid the exiles by conveying letters, etc., while if they had been allowed to
make use of the ordinary post it would have been found
much more difficult to prevail on people to convey
letters secretly. But the chief objection is that the
regulation could not possibly be thoroughly carried
out, and we know that the French never had any difficulty in carrying on a correspondence with Europe.
Countess Bertrand on the voyage home frankly stated
this to Mr. Henry,[1] and General Gourgaud before his
departure said to Major Gorrequer, the Governor's
Military Secretary, " I might if I wished have sent
away every week a packet to England." Captain
Ripley, of H.E.I.C. ship *Regent*, who landed at St.
Helena in May, 1819, stated that he was offered £600
if he would be the bearer of a letter from the French
to Europe. But I need not multiply instances, as the
fact is undisputed, and the French used to boast of it.
In October, 1817, Napoleon wrote some remarks upon
a speech of Lord Bathurst which had been made in the
House of Lords in answer to one of Lord Holland
moving for documents to show the treatment of
Napoleon at St. Helena. On this occasion Sir Hudson
Lowe departed from his instructions and allowed a
sealed packet to be sent to Lord Liverpool, although

[1] Henry, ii. 91.

he knew (or rather *because* he knew) that it contained complaints against himself. The French, however, scarcely appreciated the delicacy of his conduct, for at the same time they sent clandestinely a copy of the " Remarks " to be published in England on arrival. " Thus," says Mr. Forsyth, " the poison of calumny was disseminated abroad long before Sir Hudson Lowe ever knew, much less could reply to, the charges that were brought against him." Napoleon, it is well known, had large pecuniary resources in Europe, and it is quite possible that by correspondence he might have caused another revolution in France. We cannot, therefore, quite agree with Sir Walter Scott that the object aimed at by preventing clandestine correspondence might have been secured in some other way. It is difficult to see a way by which this object could absolutely have been attained. It was a risk that had to be run.

 (3) *That an orderly officer should be in constant attendance at Longwood, whose duty it was to see or obtain satisfactory information of Napoleon being on the spot at least twice in the twenty-four hours, and that after sunset sentries should be drawn round the house.* This regulation was made by Admiral Cockburn (except that he made the time of drawing sentries round 9 p.m.), but soon adopted by Government, as we see from a letter of Lord Bathurst, who said that they considered it a very essential point to ascertain, late in the evening and early in the morning, that Napo-

leon was safe.[1] It is obvious that there was no duty
more difficult to carry out than the instruction that
Napoleon should be seen by the orderly officer, and
yet none that was of more importance for the security
of his person. Sir Walter Scott considers that if this
order were strictly enforced nearly all the others
might have been neglected. Napoleon and his attendants at one time systematically threw every obstacle
in the way of the unfortunate orderly officer, and Sir
Hudson Lowe often had to be content with very indirect evidence of the presence of Napoleon at Longwood, and sometimes days passed without his being
seen at all. In spite of the extra pay, no officer was
willing to hold this position longer than he could help.
As to one of them (Captain Blakeney), O'Meara in his
long letter to the Admiralty stated that this officer
had long been weary of a situation in which his
" honourable feelings and sentiments were wounded
by Sir Hudson Lowe's having required him to make
a report of the conversation and action of the persons
with whom he daily sat down to table in that confidence always existing amongst brother officers."
This, however, is only one of O'Meara's misstatements. Captain Blakeney himself wrote to Count
Bertrand and stigmatized a similar statement as "false"
and an "infamous calumny," and said he resigned because his situation deprived him of the society of his
brother officers. His brother officers of the 66th also

[1] Forsyth, i. 313.

signed a declaration that they had never heard Captain Blakeney make use of any of the expressions attributed to him, or any words to that effect.[1] Matters became worse after the departure of O'Meara, who, from his position, was able to furnish the requisite information. Very amusing accounts are given by Captain Nicholls (though not perhaps so amusing to him) of the shifts to which he was put to carry out this irksome duty. He mentions being on his feet as much as ten hours at a time in order to get a glimpse of the Emperor. He says, for instance, one day that he caught a sight of him while he was strapping his razor. On another he saw the top of a cocked-hat moving about which he presumed to be Napoleon's. Once, when he applied to Count Montholon for help, the Count suggested that he could see him through the keyhole! At length Lord Bathurst lost patience, and wrote that if Napoleon's system of seclusion continued, Sir Hudson Lowe must "adopt some compulsory mode of learning a fact indispensable to the prevention of his escape."

When the Governor applied to Count Montholon on the subject, the latter replied: "It is a subject on which I cannot touch without putting him out of temper; it is the topic which irritates him most. The more I should seek to persuade him, the more obstinate he would be. He is a man who, the more cannon you fire at him, the more he resists; it is only by gentle

[1] Forsyth, iii. 118.

means that anything can be done with him." "But, Monsieur le Comte," said the Governor, "I don't fire any cannon at him; on the contrary, every one knows how far I have pushed delicacy on this subject, by refraining till now from insisting on the point." "I admit it, Monsieur le Gouverneur," replied Montholon, "and I render you full justice in this respect. The Emperor himself said, 'Well, he does his duty'; but as it is a subject on which I know he will become irritated, I had rather you would write to me, and I will send you his answer in like manner."[1] It is one thing to write despatches from Downing Street and another to carry them out at St. Helena, and in spite of all the trouble that was given on this point, Sir Hudson Lowe never did have recourse to any compulsory measure. As to the posting of sentinels after sunset, Lord Bathurst made an effective answer to Lord Holland's complaint on that head. He said in his speech:

"Sentinels were stationed there after sunset, and Napoleon had expressed his dislike to walk when he was thus watched. Sir H. Lowe, with every desire to attend to his wishes, after that fixed the sentinels in places where they would not look on him. Would their Lordships wish these sentinels to be removed altogether, just at the time when it was most likely that he should escape? Let them suppose for a moment

[1] Forsyth, iii. 67.

that, instead of debating on the motion of the noble
Lord, intelligence was brought them by Sir Hudson
Lowe that General Bonaparte had actually escaped.
Let them suppose that, instead of sitting to discuss
whether a little more or little less restriction should
be imposed, they had thus to examine Sir Hudson
Lowe at their bar. How and when did he escape?—
In the early part of the evening, and from his garden.
Had his garden no sentinels?—The sentinels were
removed. Why were they removed?—General Bonaparte desired it—they were hurtful to his feelings;
they were then removed, and thus was he enabled to
escape. What would their Lordships think of such an
answer? He begged them to consider the situation of
Sir Hudson Lowe, in what a painful and invidious
station he was placed. If General Bonaparte escaped,
the character and fortune of Sir Hudson Lowe were
ruined for ever; and if no attempts were made to
effect that escape, there would not be wanting some,
from false motives of compassion, to reproach him for
those restrictions which had probably prevented those
attempts from being made." [1]

(4) *That the best house on the island should be assigned to Napoleon, with the exception of Plantation
House, the country residence of the Governor.* It may
be admitted at once that it would have been better if
Plantation House could have been given up to Napo-

[1] Speech in the House of Lords, March 18th, 1817.

leon; but it was one of the conditions on which the East India Company allowed the use of the island to the Government, that, when Napoleon arrived, all the public buildings on it were to be at the selection of Sir George Cockburn as a residence for the Emperor, the *Governor's (Plantation House) excepted.*[1] One sufficient reason for this is plain. Plantation House was the centre of the telegraphs or semaphores of the island.[2] Sir Hudson Lowe therefore had merely to carry out orders previously enjoined on Admiral Cockburn. The latter had selected Longwood as being not only the best, but the only place on the island suitable for the residence of Napoleon.[3] Longwood was the country house of the Lieutenant-Governor. Much was done to improve it while Napoleon was at the Briars, but it was never a suitable house for him and his attendants. Materials were therefore sent out from England for the purpose of constructing a new house. When the materials came to hand, Sir Hudson Lowe

[1] Forsyth, 1. 216.

[2] See the mem. of General Beatson quoted by Dr. Rose in " Owens College Historical Essays," p. 504: "A great acquisition has lately resulted from an admirable establishment of telegraphs. These are placed upon the most commanding heights, and are so connected and so spread all over the island that no vessel can approach without being descried at the distance of sixty miles. Nothing can pass in any part, or even in sight of the island, without being instantly known to the Governor. . . . In short, the whole island can be under arms at a moment's warning. . . ."

[3] Forsyth, 1. 32.

wrote to Napoleon asking whether he would like to
have a new house erected, or additions made to the
old one. Receiving no answer, the Governor went
personally to wait upon the Emperor and obtain his
decision. The only answer he could get was that the
Emperor would prefer a new house, but that it would
take five or six years to build, and he knew he would
not be so long on the island. Sir Hudson Lowe then
proceeded to make alterations in the old house, but
Napoleon disapproved of this, though it was done for
the purpose of lodging his attendants. One cannot
object, of course, to Napoleon's having a choice either
of the new house or the old one, or between alterations
and no alterations; but the objection is that he made
every attempt to improve his residence the foundation
of a charge against Sir Hudson Lowe, and that he
watched the moment when attention was being paid
to his wishes to make that attention a source of complaint. For the summer of 1817, with a view to secure
Napoleon's comfort, Sir Hudson Lowe applied to
Miss Mason, a lady who lived at a house called Pleasant Mount, which had shady trees and water. She
was willing to let it for £100 a month, and Sir Hudson
Lowe at once wrote to Count Bertrand stating the
advantages of the situation, and telling him that if
Napoleon would accept the house it was at his disposal for the summer months. *To this letter no answer
was ever returned.* At length, when it was obvious
that there was no prospect of his recall, Napoleon did

[To face p. 172.

1 BILLIARD ROOM. 2 DRAWING-ROOM. 3 BEDROOM. 4 BATH-ROOM. 4a VALET'S ROOM.

4a

LONGWOOD, ST. HELENA. From a sketch by Lieut.-Colonel Basil Jackson.

From Forsyth's "History of the Captivity of Napoleon."

condescend to examine plans for a new house, which was actually completed a short time before his death, though, in consequence of his illness, never occupied by him. There was an iron railing some distance from the house, of the simple kind that is often put up before houses in England. It could not be seen from the house, but Napoleon took a dislike to it and said it formed an "iron cage." Sir Hudson Lowe immediately ordered it to be discontinued, and, subsequently ascertaining that the objection was not so much against the railing itself as against its too great proximity to the house, he had it placed further back. Near the end of his life Napoleon conveyed to Sir Hudson Lowe through Count Montholon his thanks to the British Government for having caused such a house to be built for him, and to Sir Hudson Lowe himself for the pains he had taken in its construction.

(5) *That certain limits should be assigned within which Napoleon should be at liberty to walk or ride unattended, but outside of them he must be accompanied by a British officer.* The general state of siege which prevailed at St. Helena has often been described. Balmain's account is as good and as short as any, so it may be reproduced here.

" As it is scarcely possible," he says, " to give a description of St. Helena different from those already known in Europe, I will only repeat that it is the dullest and the most inaccessible spot in the world, the easiest to defend, the most difficult to attack, the most expensive, and above all the most suitable for the present purpose. Such is the general idea to be formed of it.

" Every outside attack upon this island is impracticable—I think I can already say that much. Nature has imposed the first and greatest obstacles, and the English Government constantly adds fresh means of defence, the greater part of which seems to be useless. Three regiments of infantry, five companies of artillery, and a detachment of dragoons to serve a pretty large staff, form the larger portion of the garrison. Two frigates, one of them of fifty guns, several brigs and sloops guard the sea. The number of cannon placed round the coast and in the interior of the island is something alarming.

" Sir Hudson Lowe has promised to send me one of these days an account of his troops as well as the military plan of the island, and I will annex them to my next report. The strictest discipline is established at all points for the direct and indirect surveillance of Bonaparte. During the day it is not allowed to walk in certain parts without the Governor's passport. At night the password is necessary to go anywhere. In whatever direction you turn, you see nothing but sentries, pickets, and patrols. The ex-Emperor occupies at Longwood the country house of the Lieutenant-Governor. A space of several miles in circuit is at his disposal. Within it he enjoys perfect freedom.

The sentries only draw near after dark and surround the house till the morning. If he wishes to pass beyond this inclosure, which is always surrounded by troops and encampments, and defended by a park of artillery, he is followed by an officer who does not lose sight of him. Those who wish to enter, no matter how or why, must be furnished with a permit.

" At sea the regulations are still stricter. The day on which our vessel appeared before St. James's roads, one of the batteries of the fort fired a 25-pounder at us because Admiral Malcolm had omitted to send some one ashore to announce our arrival. After the evening gun no vessel can go out or stir. There are officers specially charged with knowing them and guarding them during the night. This state of things has deprived St. Helena of a great means of subsistence —fishing. It can only be carried on in the daytime, and fish is becoming as rare as fresh meat." [1]

Under Sir George Cockburn a circuit of twelve miles was allowed within which Napoleon might walk or ride unattended, while he might go anywhere on the island attended by a British officer. Surely the limit of twelve miles was ample. [2] It is true that for a time Sir Hudson Lowe made some modification in this arrangement, but as this is a matter rather personal to

[1] Balmain in " Revue Bleue," 1897, vol. vii. p. 580.
[2] St. Helena is about the size of Jersey. St. Helena, 10 m. by 8 m., area 47 sq. m. ; Jersey, 11 m. by $5\frac{1}{2}$ m., area 45 sq. m.

the Governor than connected with his instructions from home, I will deal with it later. The limits to be fixed were left to the Governor, the Government only stipulating that there should be some limits, and that these should be reasonable.

The precautions taken do seem to have erred on the side of excess, but it is difficult to enter into the feelings of the time. The people of this country were willing to credit "old Boney" with almost diabolical powers. The Duke of Wellington twenty years later considered that less elaborate measures would have been quite as effective.

"If I had been Lord Bathurst," he said, "I would have adopted a different plan for his confinement. There are only very few landing-places along the coast of St. Helena. These I would have strictly guarded, and insisted upon his showing himself to an English officer every night and morning, and then for the rest of the time I would have let him do [whatever] or go wherever he pleased. This would have avoided most matters of dispute, and then he might have received or sent as many letters as he chose." [1]

These were the principal instructions of the British Government. With regard to the first three, Sir Hudson Lowe actually relaxed them, and had to defend his conduct to the home authorities for so doing. As

[1] Stanhope's "Notes of Conversations with the Duke of Wellington," p. 104.

to the fourth, Napoleon at last admitted the pains which the Governor took to consult his comfort. The fifth is postponed for the moment. And yet all that was done was made a ground of complaint. If Sir Hudson Lowe carried out his instructions he was "tyrannical." If he ever relaxed them he was "capricious." On this point the Governor wrote not without dignity and pathos: "When you have found me accused of some atrocious cruelty, harshness, or injustice, be assured such has not merely not been committed, but that it is more than probable I have been guilty of some act of indulgence or attention on the very occasion diametrically opposite to that of which I have been accused."[1]

[1] From an unpublished letter.

N

CHAPTER X

CASE AGAINST LOWE

THE charges against Sir Hudson Lowe not so immediately connected with his instructions, and of a personal rather than an official nature, may now be considered. None of them present much difficulty.

(1) *That Napoleon was on comparatively good terms with Sir George Cockburn, and that therefore it must have been the fault of Sir Hudson Lowe that Napoleon took such a vehement dislike to him.* After the Admiral left this was constantly said by Napoleon and his attendants, but as long as he was there Napoleon could hardly say anything bad enough about him. The language in which Napoleon anticipated the arrival of Sir Hudson Lowe has been already quoted. When the Admiral refused to forward sealed packets to England, Napoleon burst out:

178

"Who is the Admiral? I never heard his name mentioned as conquering in a battle, either singly or in general action. 'Tis true he has rendered his name infamous in America, which I heard of, and he will now render it so here on this detestable rock. I believe, however, that he is a good sailor. Next to your Government exiling me here, the worst thing they could have done, and the most insufferable to my feelings, is sending me with such a man as *him*!"[1]

At another time he is represented as saying:

"In fact, I expect nothing less from your Government than that they will send out an executioner to despatch me. They send me here to a horrible rock, where even the water is not good; they send out a *sailor* with me who does not know how to treat a man like me, and who puts a *camp* under my nose, so that I cannot put my head out without seeing my jailers. Here we are treated like felons; a proclamation issued for nobody to come near or touch us, as if we were so many lepers or had the itch!"[2]

Napoleon's feeling against the Admiral is also shown by the fact that he attributed the choice of an unusually early hour for the first interview with Sir

[1] From a letter of O'Meara to Finlaison, dated March 16th, 1816, given in Forsyth, i. 66 foll.
[2] *Ibid.*

Hudson Lowe to a desire on Sir George Cockburn's part to embroil him with the new Governor. It was plainly the object of Napoleon and his suite to play off Sir Hudson Lowe against Sir George Cockburn, and when the latter had gone, then Sir George Cockburn against Sir Hudson Lowe. As a fact, Admiral Cockburn had really been wanting in courtesy to Napoleon. He had ostentatiously remained covered in his presence, and had taken a seat uninvited simply in order to assert his equality with the Emperor. His remark in the Emperor's hearing that he believed "the General had never read Chesterfield" was a rudeness of which Sir Hudson Lowe was incapable; and his reply to a letter from Bertrand that "he was not aware of an Emperor being on the island" was the merest affectation. And yet it is clear that Napoleon disliked Cockburn much less than he did Lowe, for when Admiral Malcolm (with whom Napoleon was always on good terms) slightly reproached the Emperor for his conduct towards the Governor, telling him that he misunderstood his character, the former admitted that he had behaved badly, adding, "in short, he cannot please me; call it *enfantillage* or what you will, so it is; Cockburn never vexed me with trifles."[1] In his article "Colonel Wilks and Napoleon,"[2] Mr. Julian Corbett has shown how from the moment of his arrival Sir Hudson Lowe was met

---

[1] Lady Malcolm's "Diary," p. 38; Balmain, p. 582.

[2] "Monthly Review," January, 1901.

with a declaration of war. On the day before Colonel
Wilks left (April 20th, 1816), Bertrand asked him if
he would take home a communication from Napoleon
without Lowe's seeing it. Colonel Wilks of course refused, and took as serious a view of the matter as Sir
Hudson Lowe did. This incident would not tend to
lull the suspicions of the new Governor, who, it must
be remembered, was a suspicious man by nature.

(2) *That Sir Hudson Lowe innovated upon the arrangements made by Sir George Cockburn and frequently even changed his own regulations.* This is what
has caused Sir Walter Scott, writing on imperfect information, to speak of the Governor's "want of steadiness of purpose," and if it were really the case that
the Governor *did* frequently alter his regulations he
would certainly have shown himself to be an unfit
person for the important post he occupied. But let
us look at facts. Sir Hudson Lowe did, it is true,
make some alteration in the arrangements made by
Admiral Cockburn, and not unreasonably. In July,
1816, Lord Bathurst wrote to him giving information
of certain attempts at escape that were said to have
been projected, and urging, in consequence, additional
precautions. Whether escape was possible or not—
and to us at this distance of time it may seem impossible, and additional precautions only to be lu-
dicrous—we must remember that the real question is
rather, had the British Government good ground for
suspecting the existence of such projects? There can

be no doubt that they had. Forsyth mentions certain schemes, but there was another one, apparently unknown to Forsyth, of a much more definite nature. It was hatched in the United States, where Joseph Bonaparte was then residing, and particulars of it are given in a despatch in the Foreign Office Records (France, No. 123), dated August, 1816,[1] which is directed to be sent to Sir Pulteney Malcolm and to Sir Hudson Lowe, and so, reaching the latter early in October, may have given occasion to the regulations of the 9th of October, 1816.

In Sir George Cockburn's time the sentinels were drawn round the house at 9 p.m. Now, as there was (on an average) an interval of three hours between sunset and 9 o'clock, and as this interval gave an opportunity for eluding the vigilance of the guards, Sir Hudson Lowe had the sentinels posted at sunset; but, with that deference to the susceptibilities of Napoleon which he always manifested, the sentinels were drawn only round the garden at sunset, and not round the house till nine. This regulation was bitterly resented, but was so evidently advisable that it was never relaxed. Again, it had been permitted by Sir George Cockburn that passes signed by Bertrand only should give access to Longwood, and also that invitations to dinner sent by Count Bertrand to any person who had been presented to Napoleon should

---

[1] The despatch is given by Dr. Holland Rose in "Owens College Historical Essays," p. 510.

ST HELENA

N.

...rn Point

LEMON VALLEY

King and Queen

Horse Pasture Point

Gill Point

Thompson Valley

Man and Horse Point

...leon
...de or
...much
...d Pink.
...Dec. 26.
...Blue.

MANATE BAY

2

...nford's Geog.l Estab.t London.

be received by the guard as a pass. It was obvious
that this permission was liable to abuse, and that
under cover of it sealed communications might pass.
And so it proved, for Count Bertrand soon asserted
that Sir George Cockburn had authorized a sealed
correspondence. Sir George Cockburn himself told
Sir Hudson Lowe that if he had foreseen that Count
Bertrand's house at Longwood would have been so
long in construction (he lived at first at Hutt's Gate,
about one mile from Longwood) he would not have
allowed this latitude. Sir Hudson Lowe put a stop
to this permission given to Bertrand, and made the
regulation that "persons who, with General Bonaparte's acquiescence, may at any time receive passes
from the Governor to visit him, cannot use such passes
to communicate with the other members of his family,
unless it is so specifically expressed in them."[1] This
was of much greater importance since the arrival of
the foreign Commissioners. As we have seen, the
limits within which Napoleon could ride or walk unattended had a circumference of about twelve miles,
while in the company of a British officer he could go
all over the island ; but of this permission he only
availed himself two or three times. Napoleon had never
made use of a certain road beyond a ravine which contained several houses. Sir Hudson Lowe cut off this
road, and consequently the ravine, from the boundaries,
having been informed that the inhabitants had been

[1] Forsyth, i. 331.

tampered with. It was a mistake to cut off any portion, because any harm that might be caused by conversing with the inhabitants would be more than counterbalanced by the apparent hardship inflicted, and no subsequent relaxation could altogether make up for the bad impression thus created. And there was very much relaxation, for all further changes were entirely in Napoleon's favour. After the departure of Las Cases the strict enforcement of these limits was no longer insisted on. In October, 1817, the old limits of Cockburn were not merely restored but enlarged, and in December, 1819, they were very much extended, so that even Montholon admitted the courtesy and consideration shown by the Governor for a good while past.[1] These are all the changes that were made by Sir Hudson Lowe, and it will be seen that they were made partly in order to comply more strictly with definite instructions, partly, at a later period, to mitigate, as far as he could, the inconvenience of the exiles' situation by extending their limits.

(3) *That Sir Hudson Lowe was violent in temper and coarse in language.* These charges are made against the Governor, especially as regards his interviews with Napoleon. From what has been written on this subject it might be thought that Sir Hudson Lowe was in the habit of riding to Longwood once or twice a week for the purpose of abusing and maltreating the captive Emperor. But, as already remarked, there

[1] Forsyth, iii. 236.

were only five interviews between them altogether, all in the first four months of a period of five years, and it was only at the last three of them that any stormy scenes occurred. The third interview was mostly taken up by Napoleon with abuse of Sir Hudson Lowe, and he admitted afterwards to Las Cases: " I behaved very ill to him no doubt. However, the Governor proved himself very insensible to my severity; his delicacy did not seem wounded by it. I should have liked to have seen him evince a little anger or pull the door violently after him when he went away." In other words, as Mr. Forsyth puts it, the Governor behaved with dignity and forbearance during this explosion of bad temper on the part of Napoleon. The fourth interview was much of the same nature as the third, Napoleon spending most of it in abuse; but the fifth and last, on August 18th, 1816, was an extraordinary exhibition of Napoleon's manners. He positively exhausted the vocabulary of insult and vituperation. At this interview Admiral Sir Pulteney Malcolm was present, and the Emperor had recourse to the peculiarly irritating trick of abusing a man in his presence but in language addressed to a third person, for nearly all that he said was addressed to the Admiral. It was at this interview that he called Sir Hudson a *sbirro Siciliano* (a Sicilian thieftaker).[1] Napoleon himself afterwards

[1] Sir Hudson Lowe gives a detailed account of this interview (Forsyth, i. 246-251), and if it had stood alone it might be thought too favourable to himself, but it is confirmed in all

admitted that his own conduct had been as offensive as possible, and had the justice to acknowledge that Sir Hudson Lowe had never shown him any want of respect, and that the only thing noticeable was the abrupt way in which he had retired, while the Admiral withdrew with numerous salutations. And this is all, that after being subjected to a torrent of unmerited abuse Sir Hudson Lowe withdrew without a bow! The coolness with which the Governor bore his insults increased Napoleon's anger, for he said: "This is the second time in my life that I have spoilt my affairs with the English. Their phlegm leads me on and I say more than I ought."[1] It was at this interview that the Governor is said to have laid his hand on his sword—a fable which not only Sir Hudson Lowe indignantly denied, but of which O'Meara also says that he knew it to be incorrect. The real grievance of Napoleon was clearly that he could not make the Governor lose command of his temper—that his demeanour was imperturbable. It is perfectly true that, as Lord Bathurst reminded Sir Hudson Lowe, no language of Napoleon, in the situation in which he was, could be regarded as an insult; but, however much that may be the case, things can be said which it requires extraordinary self-control not to resent. Napoleon was of course fully aware of this, and used

particulars by Admiral Malcolm. See Lady Malcolm's "Diary," pp. 53 foll.

[1] "Leur flegme me laisse aller" (Forsyth, i. 256).

his privilege to the full. Admiral Malcolm concludes
his account of the interview thus:

"During this conversation Sir Hudson never for a
moment lost his temper; Bonaparte frequently, particularly when he addressed Sir Hudson. . . . So soon
as the Admiral and Sir Hudson were gone, Bonaparte
as usual repeated all that he had said to his suite, and
they told his speeches again to various people, so that
in two days they were circulated amongst a great pro-
portion of the island, whilst the knowledge of Sir
Hudson's replies, which did him much credit, was
confined to a very small number, who were prevented
from circulating them, from the desire of the Governor
that every transaction at Longwood should be secret."[1]

In July, 1817, when Admiral Plampin replaced
Admiral Malcolm, Sir Hudson Lowe made a marked
advance to Napoleon by writing to Bertrand that if
he did not propose to introduce the new Admiral
himself, it was not from want of courtesy, but from an
idea that an introduction through Admiral Malcolm
would be more agreeable. Bertrand did not respond to
these overtures.

It is admitted by his son that Sir Hudson Lowe's
temper was *naturally* "violent and hasty enough"[2]—
all the greater credit to him then for his admirable

[1] Lady Malcolm's "Diary," p. 65.
[2] Memoir, "United Service Magazine," June, 1844.

self-control. It is right to state that in an unpublished memorandum made long after, Sir Hudson Lowe writes: "It is but justice to Napoleon to observe that he was never so very coarse and rude in his manner or language as he has been represented to have been: many a lie has thus been fathered upon him." Finally, to dispose of these charges, I will quote from a letter of Colonel Jackson to Mr. Henry, provoked by Mr. Henry's having, in his first edition, made some remark about Sir Hudson Lowe's temper on the authority of O'Meara, which in the second edition he withdrew on ascertaining that O'Meara's statement was unworthy of credit, while at the same time he says for himself, during four years' acquaintance with Sir Hudson Lowe, "the demeanour of this much-injured man was always gentlemanly and courteous, both to myself and all around him." Colonel Jackson writes as follows:

"Few persons, if any, are better acquainted with Sir Hudson Lowe than myself. When he was Quartermaster-General in 1814 and 1815, I was Deputy Assistant in the Department and attached to the office, when I was with him every day, and had indeed more communication with him than others, and sometimes of a confidential character. I also at that time saw him when certain circumstances gave him much annoyance; but cannot recollect any single instance of his breaking out into any unseemly bursts of anger, or showing real uncourteousness. He was very much liked by all who served under him, being at all times kind, considerate, generous, and hospitable. . . . Depend upon it the reports spread of Sir Hudson Lowe's 'bursts of undignified and reprehensible passion' were wholly without foundation as regards the persons at Longwood, and most grossly exaggerated as regards ourselves. I have heard Sir George Bingham speak highly of Sir Hudson; your friend, General Nicol, do the same, and, in fact, most of the officers of rank who were at St. Helena, and I cannot remember to have heard any one complain of Sir Hudson's temper. Like other men, he is liable to the infirmities of our nature; but want of proper self-command has never been one of his defects." [1]

Even Sir Walter Scott (in his "Life of Napoleon"), whom no one would ever accuse of unwillingness to do justice to the reputation of another, or suspect of unfairness in the use of materials placed at his disposal, considers that Sir Hudson Lowe failed in "proper command of temper in his intercourse with Napoleon," and in "steadiness of purpose." On the second point enough has already been said. As to the charge against Sir Hudson Lowe's temper, we must remember that Sir Walter had not the materials for a complete defence. This required an inspection of the minutes made by Major Gorrequer of the conversations held, a comparison of O'Meara's printed narra-

[1] Henry, ii. 59 n.

tive with his private letters, and the consideration of many documents in Sir Hudson Lowe's possession which Sir Walter Scott had no opportunity of perusing. Moreover, at the time he wrote, Sir Hudson Lowe was in Ceylon, and could not personally, therefore, be consulted. It is, however, impossible to suppose that Sir Walter can have attentively read the correspondence between Lord Bathurst and the Governor of St. Helena, and the other official documents, and weighed their evidence against that of such authors as O'Meara, Las Cases, and Antommarchi. In them there is not a line to warrant the conclusion that Sir Hudson Lowe ever regarded Napoleon as " an object of resentment, and open to retort and retaliation." Sir Archibald Alison's language is more unfavourable. He says: "Sir Hudson Lowe, who was appointed to the military command of the island, proved an unhappy selection. His manner was rigid and unaccommodating, and his temper of mind was not such as to soften the distress which the Emperor endured during his detention."[1] Lord Campbell is still more condemnatory in his " Life of Lord Eldon." He says: "As things were managed, I am afraid it will be said that he [Napoleon] was treated, in the nineteenth century, with the same cruel spirit as the Maid of Orleans was in the fifteenth; and there may

[1] "History of Europe, 1789-1815," xiv. 194. It is but fair to add that, after reading Forsyth, Alison uses much milder language in his "History of Europe, 1815-1852," ii. 370.

be tragedies on the Death of Napoleon, in which Sir Hudson Lowe will be the *sbirro*, and even Lord Eldon may be introduced as the *stern old councillor* who decreed the hero's imprisonment."[1] But these writers had no more means of knowing the truth than what Sir Walter Scott possessed, and it is "impossible not to see that they have all been influenced in their opinions by the assertions of authors, the bitterest enemies of Sir Hudson Lowe, who had hitherto occupied the field of narrative with regard to the events at St. Helena."[2] As before remarked, all this has been, or, at least, should have been, altered since the publication of Mr. Forsyth's book, and those who now believe that Sir Hudson Lowe was guilty of harshness of temper and coarseness of language will believe almost anything.

(4) *That Sir Hudson Lowe gradually procured the dismissal of the faithful attendants of Napoleon with the intention of aggravating the prisoner's painful situation and getting him more and more into his power.* Las Cases, Gourgaud, Bertrand, and Montholon were the four principal sharers of Napoleon's exile, and they, together with the surgeon O'Meara, were those most about his person. The circumstances attending the removal of O'Meara have already been narrated, and it has been shown that Sir Hudson Lowe would have endeavoured to procure his removal at an earlier period,

---

[1] "Lives of the Chancellors," vii. 321.

[2] Forsyth, i. 125.

had it not been that he was unwilling to remove one
to whom the Emperor seemed attached. At the close
of 1816 Las Cases was sent away owing to the dis-
covery of unauthorized communications by him. There
is no need to go into the details, as they are not in dispute. A servant of Las Cases who was going to
Europe was accidentally discovered to have a letter
concealed in the lining of his waistcoat. But it is very
doubtful whether Las Cases, in spite of his protesta-
tions, had any objection to leave Longwood. He had
to sail first to the Cape of Good Hope, in accordance
with the instructions from England that those who left
St. Helena should go first to the Cape, and, in the interval before a ship was ready for him, Sir Hudson
Lowe gave him the option of returning to Longwood.
Of this he never availed himself, although Bertrand
called upon him in order to urge it.[1] O'Meara says,
in a letter to Finlaison, that in his opinion Las Cases
had planned the whole scheme on purpose to be
detected, being heartily tired of his residence in the
island; in other words, that (in sporting language)
" he was riding for a fall."[2] The evidence may not go
so far as this, but it is hardly uncharitable to suppose
with Colonel Jackson that he was "very glad to get
out of the mess,"[3] in spite of the fact that he was

[1] Forsyth, ii. 41.

[2] Count Balmain mentions this view as prevalent on the
island (Balmain, p. 619).

[3] Henry, ii. 47.

genuinely attached to his master. Sir Hudson Lowe gave Las Cases a friendly letter of introduction to Lord Charles Somerset, Governor of the Cape of Good Hope, who thus wrote back some time afterwards, when the " Journal " had been published:

" The whole of the Count's publication (if it really be his) is so contemptible a performance that I own his wailings and his complaints, as far as they involve myself, are matters perfectly indifferent to me; with regard to his assertions respecting the Cape and his treatment here, I know them to be so absolutely and impudently false that it is not too much to presume that there is not a single correct statement in the whole book." [1]

In the beginning of 1818 General Gourgaud of his own accord applied for leave to return to Europe, which was granted. For a long time Napoleon had ceased to be cordial to him. Owing to his extremely jealous affection for the Emperor he was in open enmity with Montholon (to whom he actually sent a challenge) and saw only the Bertrands.

" I used," says Colonel Jackson, " frequently to call and chat with him, when he would often lament his hard fate, and sigh for *la belle France*, for Paris and *les Boulevards*. At length *maladie de pays* got the better of him, and he determined to leave Longwood.

[1] Forsyth, iii. 148.

Sir Hudson Lowe sent for me, and, having mentioned Gourgaud's wish, asked whether it would be agreeable for me to reside with him until an opportunity should offer for his quitting St. Helena. . . . Accordingly, General Gourgaud and myself were installed in a comfortable house, in which servants and a table were provided for us at the expense of Government. We lived near the residence of the Austrian and Russian Commissioners, whom we occasionally visited, and nothing could exceed the attention and hospitality of Sir Hudson Lowe to General Gourgaud." [1]

Colonel Jackson then gives a remarkable instance of the Governor's generosity:

" In justice to that excellent and grossly maligned individual, Sir Hudson Lowe, I shall now relate a circumstance which I am sure General Gourgaud will be ready to confirm. When the latter removed from Longwood, I accompanied him to the Governor's residence, when I took an opportunity to leave him and Sir Hudson *tête-à-tête*. Immediately on our riding from Plantation House together, the General broke out into strong exclamations of surprise that Sir Hudson should simply have received his visit as the call of one gentleman upon another, without ever alluding to Longwood during their conversation. ' I expected,' added he, ' that the Governor would have seized with

[1] Henry, ii. 48.

avidity so favourable an occasion as my excited state offered to gather from me some information about the goings on at Longwood. *Je ne reviens pas de mon étonnement, non, je n'en reviens pas.* These expressions of surprise he repeated over and over again during our short ride. I may add that I had many opportunities of remarking the really chivalrous delicacy of Sir Hudson in reference to General Gourgaud.

"Although the Emperor and the General did not part the best friends, yet, as it was known at Longwood that the latter was unprovided with funds, a considerable sum was offered to him by Napoleon, and even pressed on his acceptance when leaving Longwood, which he declined to receive. But soon after, when about to embark for England, the poor General found the usual inconveniences of a penniless position, and sent me to Longwood to ask Marshal Bertrand for a loan of two or three hundred pounds. The Marshal declined, saying that the Emperor had offered him a much larger sum, the refusal of which was most disrespectful; but added that even then, if General Gourgaud would accept the Emperor's gift, he would also lend him the sum he asked.

"Gourgaud was a good deal distressed by the refusal of Bertrand, which was quite unexpected, but still declined placing himself under a pecuniary obligation to Napoleon; and would have sailed to England without a shilling but for Sir Hudson Lowe, who, as soon as he learned the circumstances, sent him by note an order for one hundred pounds on his bankers in London." [1]

While living with Jackson, Gourgaud had some strange talk with Stürmer, in which he maintained that Napoleon had plenty of means at his disposal and could escape when he liked, but that he preferred to be a prisoner at St. Helena because of the importance attached to his position: "Je ne peux plus vivre en particulier; j'aime mieux être prisonnier ici que libre aux Etats-Unis." [2] After his arrival in England Gourgaud for a time continued the same line of conduct and had interviews with Mr. Goulburn (Under-Secretary for War and the Colonies), in which he avowed that the inhabitants of Longwood had free and uninterrupted communication with Europe. [3] Upon all this Lord Rosebery remarks: "We are rather inclined to believe that either to obtain the confidence of these gentlemen [i.e., Lowe, Bathurst, or Stürmer], or to gratify his own sense of humour, or, most prob-

[1] Henry, ii. 48-50. This account is also given at greater length in Jackson's "Waterloo and St. Helena," pp. 149-156.

[2] This conversation is given in Forsyth, iii. 392-394, from Stürmer's despatch of March 14th, 1818. In Stürmer's book (p. 125) it is omitted, and a reference given to Forsyth. Montchenu claims the honour of this conversation, and gives it in identical terms with Stürmer (with one slight exception), and says that he had prepared the questions beforehand ("La Captivité de Ste.-Hélène," pp. 137-141). It seems to have taken place in the presence of both.

[3] Forsyth, iii. 38.

able of all, to divert their suspicions from something else, he was mystifying them; and, perhaps, as Montholon says, overplaying his part";[1] and he considers that Gourgaud revealed nothing of the least importance either at St. Helena or in London. Very likely not, but from any point of view the conduct of Gourgaud cannot be approved. His "revelations" were either true or untrue. In the former case he was certainly a traitor to Napoleon. In the latter his conduct was rather that of a lunatic than a humorist. From what else does Lord Rosebery think "suspicions could be diverted" by such talk? Sir Walter Scott, who could appreciate humour as well as Lord Rosebery, entirely fails to appreciate the humour of Gourgaud on this occasion, for he writes as follows upon this subject:

"General Gourgaud may represent the whole of his communications as a trick played off upon the English Ministers, in order to induce them to grant his personal liberty. But I cannot imitate the General's disregard of common civility so far as to suppose him capable of a total departure from veracity, when giving evidence upon his word of honour. In representing the ex-Emperor's health as good, his finances as ample, his means of escape as easy and frequent, while he knew his condition to be the reverse in every particular, General Gourgaud must

[1] "Napoleon: the Last Phase," p. 38.

have been sensible that the deceptive views thus impressed on the British Ministers must have had the natural effect of adding to the rigours of his patron's confinement." [1]

One of the consequences of Gourgaud's information in London was the recall of O'Meara by the Government, as we have already seen. [2]

As is well known, General Gourgaud some years later attacked Sir Walter Scott in consequence of the use made by the latter in his "Life of Napoleon" of Gourgaud's voluntary statements, but drew back at the last. The "Times," with the usual brutality of John Bull (as the French would say), summed up the situation in these words: "The aide-de-camp of St. Helena shows himself to be nothing better than a cross between a blusterer and a sophist." After his interviews with Mr. Goulburn he was, Colonel Jackson tells us, turned round again by politicians in this country in favour of Napoleon, who told him that otherwise he would be of no account. "This he did by inditing a letter to Marie Louise, in which he inveighed against the treatment of Napoleon at the hands of Government and Sir Hudson Lowe, which being duly published, Gourgaud fell to zero in the opinion of all right-minded persons." [3]

[1] Lockhart's "Life of Scott" (one-vol. ed.), p. 667.
[2] See above, p. 106.
[3] "Waterloo and St. Helena," p. 158.

Gourgaud began to forgive Montholon by borrowing money from the Countess, and in time, we read, became *un homme raisonnable*.

We have seen in Mr. Henry's narrative [1] how an attempt was made to bribe him to become *l'homme de l'Empereur*, and how, after the departure of O'Meara, early in August, 1818, Mr. Stokoe's career, as medical attendant to Napoleon, was prematurely cut short.[2] Next, Dr. Verling, of the Royal Artillery, was ordered to take up his abode at Longwood, and after a short time he too was offered a large bribe by Montholon if he would abandon the Governor and attach himself to the Emperor, as O'Meara had done. But Dr. Verling came low down on the "bribability list," drawn up by O'Meara, which Jackson tells us he saw. The Count's proposition was indignantly rejected; the doctor mounted his horse and rode to Plantation House, reported the affair to the Governor, and requested to be relieved from a post where he was liable to such an insult. He could not be relieved at the time, and remained at Longwood until the arrival of Dr. Antommarchi in September, 1819. So much then for the "removal" of Las Cases, Gourgaud, and Stokoe. Counts Bertrand and Montholon remained to the end (although the Governor had plenty of excuse for sending the former away), and they were, as we have seen, on good terms with Sir Hudson Lowe after the death of Napoleon. Bertrand afterwards was so far from sup-

[1] See above, p. 104.   [2] See above, p. 22.

porting the credit of O'Meara's book that he published in the "Constitutionnel" a letter, in which he stated it as due to the memory of Napoleon, to France, and to Europe, to declare himself an utter stranger to the conversations reported in the "Voice from St. Helena."[1]

(5) *That enough money was not allowed for the support in proper style of Napoleon and his suite, and that in consequence some of Napoleon's plate had to be broken up and sold to supply the deficiency.* If we believe Las Cases, they were in actual want of food; if we believe Napoleon himself, "there had been enough to eat supplied, though not enough to keep a proper table"; but if we look to the evidence of facts we can believe neither of them. According to the Napoleonic Legend, the Emperor said to the Governor that if sufficient food were not supplied him, he would take his seat at the table of the brave officers of the 53rd; and was certain they would not refuse a share of their dinner to an old soldier like him. This is, however, only one of those speeches that *ought* to have been made but were not, although it speedily got into circulation.[2] The orders of Government were that the table was to be supplied on the scale of a general of the first rank. Sir Hudson Lowe, finding on his arrival that the amount of £8,000 a year allowed by Government for the Longwood establishment was not sufficient, im-

---

[1] "United Service Magazine," June, 1844, p. 293.
[2] Forsyth, i. 271.

mediately, and on his own responsibility, raised it to £12,000 a year, which, if expenses had been kept within reasonable limits, would have been sufficient. Anything beyond this was defrayed by Napoleon himself. As Dr. Holland Rose remarks, "our Ministers knew that Napoleon possessed large funds that were available for means of escape; and they could scarcely be expected to tax our hard-pressed people in order to furnish the superfluities of life to a State prisoner who was likely to use that abundance against them."[1]

Personally the Emperor was not extravagant in his living, but the extravagance of his followers knew no bounds. In one of O'Meara's letters to Finlaison—the statement will be sought in vain in his book—he calls them, "except one or two, the greatest gluttons and epicures he ever saw," and he goes on to describe their style of living.[2] Each upper domestic was allowed a bottle of claret a day at the price of £6 per dozen, and the amount of wine consumed averaged two bottles a day per head for the whole establishment. The food was plentiful, but the quality sometimes left something to be desired. Colonel Jackson

---

[1] "Owens College Historical Essays," p. 514. Dr. Rose appends a note on Napoleon's expenditure for the months October, 1815, to January, 1816, which is found in our archives. It is headed "Etat des dépenses que Mr. Balcombe est autorisé à payer sur les fonds de 4,000 napoléons," and amounts to £1,757 7s.

[2] Some allowance must here be made for O'Meara's habitual exaggeration.

says: "Provisions may not have been of the highest quality, though the best the island afforded."[1] That of course is the point, and Mr. Henry humorously complains of the inferior living that the 66th Regiment had to put up with. "The superior quality," he says, "of everything used at Longwood at this time was notorious. The purveyor for that establishment found means always to monopolize the best meat; his daily cart conveying provisions to Longwood often underwent the envious scrutiny of our officers, as they met it in the course of their rides, when the peevish exclamation, 'We can't get anything like that for the mess,' was generally the result."[2] We also find Dr. Baxter, the Deputy-Inspector of Hospitals at St. Helena, requesting the Governor to interfere "in the universal and sweeping monopoly of the contractors for Longwood," and complaining that he cannot get enough milk for the sick of the 53rd Regiment. On one occasion a complaint was made that not enough coals and wood was allowed. The Governor immediately ordered the allowance of coal to be doubled, the wood to remain the same, on account of the great scarcity of wood in the island. The next time they were out of wood the French servants broke up a bedstead and some shelves for the fires at Longwood, pretending that they would not be allowed more wood. Napoleon approved of wood not being asked

---

[1] "Waterloo and St. Helena," p. 173.
[2] Henry, ii. 54 n.

for, saying he could pay for it himself. The Governor remarked, on hearing of it, that this was always the way: they never would tell what they required, and then complained of the want of it. As to breaking up the plate, as it was well known that Napoleon had plenty of ready money at his command, it was clear that this pretended sacrifice was made for the edification of the European public.[1] O'Meara in a letter to Finlaison says of Napoleon: " In this he has also a wish to excite an odium against the Governor by saying that he has been obliged to sell his plate in order to provide against starvation, *as he himself told me was his object.*" Of a second sale of plate Montholon writes: " I was to persist in saying that his [Napoleon's] plate was his only resource at St. Helena; and I received the order to have all the plate broken up, with the exception of twelve covers," thus admitting in so many words that the scheme was one to impose on the public.[2] But the pretence of ill-treatment was not always consistently kept up, and we find towards the end of the time various acknowledgements by Montholon of the

[1] See "English Historical Review," April, 1902, " Funeral of Napoleon and his Last Papers," by Dr. Rose, where Sir Hudson Lowe's list of the plate at Longwood on April 15th, 1821, is given, which shows that the sales of plate were far from depleting the store.

[2] Upon this Lord Rosebery remarks (p. 94): "We cannot refrain from a kind of admiration, both at the result and at the meagreness of his means." Perhaps not, if every means is to be considered legitimate. We might feel the same "kind of admiration" for Titus Oates, who certainly produced results.

trouble which was taken to supply them properly. Thus, in January, 1820, he said to Major Gorrequer, in reply to a question on the subject of provisions: "We can only congratulate ourselves on the manner in which we are served." It must be certainly borne in mind that the arrival of Napoleon and suite—about fifty people—much increased prices at St. Helena, which became about three or four times what they were in Europe. A great part of the reports of the Commissioners—especially of Montchenu—is taken up with complaints of their inability to keep up their proper position through want of money, and their consequent applications for an increase in allowance. Balmain says he has seen £6 paid for half a pig, and £60 asked for a dozen chairs. Montchenu gives an elaborate list of prices, in which he reckons washing and soap at £100 per annum![1]

(6) *That Napoleon was not allowed to have a regular supply of books and newspapers, and that what were sent were often detained altogether, or for some time, by Sir Hudson Lowe.* As for books, one work by Mr. Hobhouse (afterwards Lord Broughton), sent by the author to Napoleon, was, it is true, detained by the Governor, because in one volume was written "Imperatori Napoleon." It may have been good or bad judgement to detain the volumes, but the point is that in a note to Sir Hudson Lowe Mr. Hobhouse expressly authorized detention of them, "if it be thought

[1] Balmain, p. 620; "La Captivité de Ste.-Hélène," p. 16.

improper to give them at all to the person for whom they are destined." This seems to be the only case in which a book was kept back. On the other hand, £1,400 worth of books was ordered from booksellers for Napoleon and received by him. With regard to newspapers, Count Montholon writes in his " Remonstrance," which was meant for European consumption only: "We are prohibited from receiving the ' Morning Chronicle,' the ' Morning Post,' or any French papers; occasionally a few odd numbers of the ' Times' are sent to Longwood." To this the Governor replied, speaking in the third person:

" General Bonaparte once sent a message to him requesting him to send him the ' Morning Chronicle,' and he immediately sent the whole of those which he had then in his possession. No application was ever made to him to subscribe either to the ' Morning Chronicle ' or the ' Morning Post,' or to any French journals. Had such an application been made he would have made the application known to his Government. It has not been odd numbers of the ' Times' newspaper, but regular series of them, which have been constantly sent, the Governor never having kept back a single number. If any numbers were kept back it must have been done by his [Napoleon's] own followers, to whom they were always enclosed for him." [1]

[1] Forsyth, i. 267.

O'Meara too says, in his "Voice from St. Helena," with reference to newspapers received: "None except some odd numbers of the 'Times,' 'Courier,' 'Observer,' etc., with a few French papers of very old date, reached Longwood during my residence there. In one instance—in March, 1817, I think—the Governor permitted me to take the 'Morning Chronicle' for some weeks, as a great favour, which was not again repeated."[1] And yet O'Meara had written to Sir Hudson Lowe on the previous June 20th, in reply to inquiries of the Governor "to be informed of the names of such newspapers as General Bonaparte may have received." After giving the names of a good many English newspapers, he says: "*These, with the usual series of papers sent by yourself,* some French papers, and 'Morning Chronicle' for October, November, and part of December, also sent by yourself, form the whole of the newspapers he has received."[2] The doctor thus disposes of himself. Yet this entry of March 28th, 1818, is retained in the 1888 edition!

The £1,400 worth of books was never paid for by Napoleon. "So," says Lord Rosebery, "on his death the books were impounded by Lowe, and sold in London for a few hundred pounds."[3] As to whether the books were sold or not I cannot say, and Lord Rosebery gives no authority, but if they were it was certainly by order of Government. After Napoleon's

---

[1] "Voice from St. Helena," ii. 397, under March 28th, 1818.
[2] Forsyth, ii. 160.   [3] "Napoleon: the Last Phase," p. 97.

death his library consisted of about 2,700 volumes, and a list was made of his books and papers.[1] The story seems highly improbable and belongs to the Legend rather than to History.

(7) *That Sir Hudson Lowe offered inducements to O'Meara to act as a spy, and on his refusal tried to ruin him.* This charge has been already dealt with by anticipation under the general account of O'Meara. We have also seen that the Governor abstained from putting questions to General Gourgaud about Longwood at a time when he might have obtained much information. I will add what Colonel Jackson says, to show how foreign it was to the honourable nature of Sir Hudson Lowe to expect such services: " It is incumbent on me in this place distinctly to declare that Sir Hudson Lowe never breathed a word to me having reference to surveillance; and I may also state that the great delicacy observed by him on that point first inspired in me the high respect for his character which I have never since ceased to feel up to the present moment."[2] Towards people in general who visited Longwood the Governor clearly states his attitude in a letter to Sir Pulteney Malcolm, the Admiral then on the station:

"When visitors did go I was not in the habit of troubling them with interrogations, and can boldly

[1] " Eng. Hist. Review," April, 1902.
[2] " United Service Magazine," March, 1844, p. 418.

appeal to every person who has been admitted to visit at Longwood, or the Bertrands, for the delicacy I have observed on this point. I should not, however, the less expect, if anything important for me to learn was said, that it should be made known to me. If I thought reserve practised I would not hesitate to question—considering that any conversation had with General Bonaparte, or the persons of his suite, which has relation to my duties on this island, or embraces any subject of *political interest*, ought as a matter of course to be communicated to me, as well from regard to the situation I fill here as to the confidence which Government has reposed in me, being at the same time rendered by their instructions the responsible person for all conversations with him." [1]

This was an intelligible position for the Governor to maintain, and the more justifiable because of the refusal of Napoleon to hold personal intercourse with him. Whether, however, it was prudent to assume an attitude which at least seemed to be inquisitorial may be doubted, for, as above remarked, it was not enough for the Governor to be right, he had to be obviously right. With reference to a case of Sir Hudson Lowe's way of questioning on matters of public interest, and otherwise procuring information of this character, Lady Malcolm says: "The Admiral now discovered that there was a system of spies on the island, and

[1] Forsyth, ii. 128.

that every trifle was reported to the Governor. With open, candid Englishmen this is detestable, and must cause incalculable evil."[1] The context does not support the view that there was a system of spies, but the Governor's methods cannot have been quite free from objection if this remark could with plausibility be made about them.

(8) *That surreptitious bulletins were given to the Governor of Napoleon's health by a person who never saw him.* This charge is made by O'Meara,[2] and is a good example of *suppressio veri.* The explanation is simple enough. "Nothing," says Mr. Forsyth, "could be more proper than that the Governor should endeavour to obtain a second opinion as to the health and medical treatment of Napoleon from a skilful professional person, who was competent to form a judgement upon O'Meara's medical details. In reality, however, the so-called 'fictitious bulletins' were merely repetitions of the information given by O'Meara to Mr. Baxter, and the writer rarely expressed any opinion of his own." Dr. Baxter was the principal medical officer on the island, and his services had been offered by Sir Hudson to Napoleon, who refused to see him, and at the same time intimated that he distrusted any medical man in the confidence of the Governor. Dr. Baxter himself wrote on the subject as follows: " The expressions of Mr. O'Meara

[1] " Diary," p. 166.
[2] " Voice from St. Helena," ii. 398.

were scrupulously attended to in making the report to the Governor, and for the truth of the statements made by me to the Governor from these examinations I pledge myself as a man of honour. In the preamble to the report it is explicitly stated to be the substance of an examination of Mr. O'Meara touching the state of health of Napoleon Bonaparte, and does in no way imply that I was in attendance upon him."[1] It is difficult to see what there was "surreptitious" in this. No change, however, is made in the 1888 edition of O'Meara's book.

(9) *That Sir Hudson Lowe had thrown obstacles in the way of Napoleon receiving a marble bust of his son, the young Duc de Reichstadt, and had even suggested that it should be destroyed to prevent it from reaching Longwood.* O'Meara is the principal disseminator of this charge when he says: " The bust had been in the island for fourteen days, during several of which it was at Plantation House."[2] I have purposely kept this charge to the last, as it is the one that would tell (and did tell) most of all upon the British public, and if there had been any truth in it the name of Sir Hudson Lowe would be deservedly branded as that of a man wanting in all delicacy of feeling and a stranger to the natural affections. But the charge is simply untrue. *The bust was landed on the* 10th *or* 11th *of June and sent to Longwood on the next day.* As so much has

---

[1] Forsyth, ii. 261.
[2] " Voice from St. Helena," ii. 100 n.

been made of this matter, Mr. Forsyth deals with it at
some length, and supports all he says by documentary
evidence printed at the end of his second volume.
He writes as follows:

"It is not quite clear how the bust was made, but
at all events it was purchased by Messrs. Beaggini in
London in hopes that a favourable opportunity might
occur for transmitting it to St. Helena. It happened
that a vessel, the *Baring*, commanded by Captain
Lamb, was about to sail there in January, 1817, on
board of which was a foreign sailor named Rethwick,
or Radovitch, in the capacity of gunner, and to him
Messrs. Beaggini confided the bust, with instructions
that he was to endeavour to give it to Count Bertrand
for Napoleon, and to make no stipulation for any payment, but leave it to the generosity of 'the Emperor'
to refund their expense. If, however, Bonaparte wished
to know the price, he was to ask a hundred louis for
the bust. Captain Lamb had no knowledge of the
matter until shortly before, or immediately after, the
arrival of his ship at St. Helena, on May 28th. At that
time Rethwick was ill from a fit of apoplexy, which was
succeeded by delirium, so that it was for several days
impossible to speak to him on the subject. When Sir
Thomas Reade was informed that the bust was on
board, he immediately went to the Governor and acquainted him with the fact. Sir Hudson Lowe at first
hesitated as to the course which his duty required him

to take—considering the clandestine manner in which
an attempt was thus made to communicate with Napoleon—and he was inclined not to allow the bust to
be forwarded until he had communicated with Lord
Bathurst on the subject. Sir Thomas Reade, however,
suggested that, as the bust was made of marble and not
plaster, so that it could not possibly contain anything
improper, it might be forwarded to Longwood at once,
and, as its arrival had already become known, Sir
Hudson assented to the proposal. Before, however,
ordering it to be sent on shore, he went on June 10th
to Longwood to communicate with Count Bertrand
and ascertain Napoleon's wishes. Major Gorrequer
accompanied him, and he gives in his Minutes the following account of the interview:

"'The Governor called on Count Bertrand (whither
I attended him), and informed him that in the store-
ship (the *Baring*) was a marble bust said to be that of
the young Napoleon; that it appeared it was brought
out by an under-officer of the ship; that, although it
had come in a very irregular manner, yet, under the impression that it might be a thing acceptable "*à celui
qui résidait à Longwood*," he would take upon himself
the responsibility of landing it, if such was his wish;
that he requested Count Bertrand would make it
known, and inform him if he wished to have it, and it
would be brought on shore. He answered, "*Oh! sans
doute, que ça lui fera plaisir; envoyez-le toujours.*" The
Governor added, the man in whose charge it came was

ill, in fact delirious, and it was impossible to speak to him on the subject. All he knew about it would be found in the two papers (one a letter, the other a memorandum) which he handed over to the Count, who read them (they were in Italian) and returned them. After leaving the house, the Governor went back (I following), and again gave the two papers to the Count, that he might show them to General Bonaparte, begging he afterwards would return them to him, and told Count Bertrand he would have the bust landed the following day.'

"The next day the bust was landed and sent up to Longwood, when Bonaparte received it with evident satisfaction and delight. He had, however, been informed of its arrival (how it does not appear) some days previously. On the 10th he had said to O'Meara: ' I have known of it for several days. I intended, if it had not been given, to have made such a complaint as would have caused every Englishman's hair to stand on end with horror. I would have told a tale which would have made the mothers of England execrate him as a monster in human shape.' No one can doubt this, for there was no lack of willingness or of ability for the purpose; but unfortunately for the well-conceived plot of the story the Governor did not give him the opportunity. But Napoleon persisted in believing, or affecting to believe, that the latter had originally given orders for the destruction of the bust, telling O'Meara, who endeavoured to convince him of the contrary, 'that it was in vain to attempt to deny a known fact'; and upon this imaginary hypothesis he broke out into a violent tirade against Sir Hudson Lowe, calling him barbarous and atrocious. 'That countenance,' he exclaimed, gazing at the marble image of his son, 'would melt the heart of the most ferocious wild beast. The man who gave orders to break that image would plunge a knife into the heart of the original if it were in his power.'"[1]

Subsequently Count Bertrand had an interview with Captain Lamb, and asked him whether the Governor had not intended to keep back the bust altogether, and whether he had not spoken of breaking it to pieces. To this Captain Lamb very properly replied that if Sir Hudson Lowe had intended to keep it back he need only have mentioned his wish to him, when of course it would not have been landed. The sailor who brought it received a cheque for £300 from the Emperor. Of him O'Meara says: "By means of some unworthy tricks the poor man did not receive the money for nearly two years." The fact is, however, that the man turned out to be a great scamp. He received the money and would not return any of it to Messrs. Beaggini, who, about a year and eight months afterwards, wrote to Count Bertrand to inform him of the conduct of Radovitch, and to solicit some remuneration for themselves. It will hardly be believed that

[1] Forsyth, ii. 146-149.

this atrocious charge against Sir Hudson Lowe is retained unaltered in the 1888 edition of O'Meara's book, in spite of the exposure of its falsehood by Mr. Forsyth.[1] At a later period Sir Hudson Lowe received a despatch from Lord Bathurst containing the Prince Regent's approval of his conduct in sending to Napoleon the bust of his son. But Lord Bathurst added: " The suspicious circumstances, however, under which it arrived at St. Helena, as detailed in your despatch, were sufficient to make you pause before you determined to transmit it to the General. Had the package contained anything less interesting to him in his private character as a father, the clandestine manner in which it appears to have been introduced on board the vessel would have been a sufficient reason for withholding the delivery of it, at least for a much longer period." The Government therefore, while approving Sir Hudson Lowe's conduct in this matter, evidently considered that he needed a warning against showing too much leniency.

The chief specific charges against Sir Hudson Lowe have now been stated, and it is time to look a little at the other side of the picture, to show not merely that he was not guilty of any of the atrocities of which he has been so recklessly accused, but that he was a man

---

[1] Mr. Watson also, faithful to the Legend, remarks: "The bust of the King of Rome came also, and this was long held by Lowe, who threatened to break it in pieces" ("Napoleon," p. 679).

remarkable for delicacy, generosity, and humanity. To his delicacy Mr. Henry bears witness in the following striking passage:

"It is extremely probable, and I believe it to be a fact, that Sir Hudson Lowe went to St. Helena determined to conduct himself with courtesy and kindness to Napoleon, and to afford him as many comforts and as much personal freedom as were consistent with his safe custody. I was intimately acquainted with the officer charged with the care of Longwood for nearly three years, and he assured me that the Governor repeatedly desired him to consult the comfort of the great man and his suite, to attend to their suggestions, and to make their residence as agreeable as possible. Two of the orderly officers at Longwood, namely, Majors Blakeney and Nicholls of the 66th Regiment, have given me the same assurance. I have myself seen courteous notes from Sir Hudson Lowe to these officers, accompanying pheasants and other delicacies sent from Plantation House for Napoleon's table. Even after two unfortunate interviews, when the Emperor worked himself into a rage and used gross and insulting expressions to the Governor, evidently to put him into a passion, but without success (for Sir Hudson maintained perfect self-possession and self-command throughout), even after this open breach the above civilities were not discontinued. Still, when a pheasant, the greatest rarity in the island, appeared on the Governor's table, one was sure to be sent to Longwood."[1]

A little further on the same writer says:

"During my residence at St. Helena opportunities of observing minutely the character of Sir Hudson Lowe were not wanting, and I believe nobody could fill all the ordinary relations of domestic life and of society better than this much calumniated man. He was to my certain knowledge a kind husband and father, and I believe an excellent magistrate and civil governor."[2]

I have mentioned acts of courtesy on the part of Sir Hudson Lowe to Countess Bertrand.[3] There was no reason to complain of her demeanour or of that of Countess Montholon during their stay at St. Helena. Countess Bertrand was a lady of much spirit and wit. Mr. Henry frequently lets us see how highly he thought of her. One of her witty remarks is preserved amid the constant tale of bickering. She was confined in January, 1817, and some days afterwards, when Napoleon paid her a visit, she said to him: "Sire, I have the honour to present to your Majesty *le premier Français* who, since your arrival, has entered Longwood without Lord Bathurst's permission." The child

---

[1] Henry, ii. 57.   [2] See Appendix C.
[3] Madame Bertrand was a Creole. Her father, General Arthur Dillon, was an Irishman in the French service who perished in the Revolution.

was named after the Emperors of Austria and Russia and the Duke of Wellington. When a letter arrived announcing the death of the Countess's mother, Sir Hudson Lowe sent it with a note to Count Bertrand from himself, so that the news might be broken gently to her. No one could have acted with more delicacy; yet because, nearly a year afterwards, the Countess received a letter brought by a person who came out as governess to her children, speaking of the death of her mother as a long past event, he is, under the head of "Brutal conduct of Sir Hudson Lowe to the Countess Bertrand," accused by O'Meara of little less than a design upon her life in having suffered the letter to reach her![1] Again, when a newspaper arrived which contained an announcement that Count Bertrand had been condemned *par contumace* for high treason, Sir Hudson Lowe caused the paper to be sent separately to the Count with a private note, for fear the news might first meet the eye of the Countess. At another time, when a newspaper mentioned the death of one of Count Montholon's children, the Governor inclosed the paper with a note to the Abbé Buonavita, whom he considered the proper person to break the information to Count Montholon. These are indeed remarkable instances of coarse-mindedness and brutality on the

[1] O'Meara's "Exposition," pp. 152, 153. This was a publication sent out by O'Meara to St. Helena in 1819; a sort of skeleton outline, afterwards filled out to the proportions of the "Voice from St. Helena."

Governor's part![1] Let it be noticed also how some of his civilities were received. Early in July, 1817, there arrived at St. Helena a beautiful set of chessmen, two workboxes, and some other articles of Chinese manufacture as a present to Napoleon from the Hon. John Elphinstone, as a mark of gratitude to the Emperor for having saved the life of his brother, Captain Elphinstone, who was severely wounded and made prisoner on the day before Waterloo. Mr. Forsyth thus writes:

"The letter that accompanied them was immediately forwarded to Longwood, with an intimation that the articles would follow. On examining them it was discovered that the presents were marked with eagles and the initial N surmounted by the imperial crown, a recognition or allusion to his former rank which rendered them under the regulations inadmissible. Sir Hudson Lowe, however, transmitted the articles; but he thought it right to advert to the irregularity, and wrote to Bertrand, saying that if he were to act in strict conformity with the established rules he ought to delay sending them; but that, as he had promised that the boxes should follow the letter, he had no alternative but to forward them."[2]

[1] Mr. Watson still gives us the Legend: "If Lowe happened upon some peculiarly bitter weed of abuse of Napoleon, that was sent up to Longwood. If books, papers, or magazines arrived in which he was tenderly handled, such articles rarely reached the lonely man they would have cheered" ("Napoleon," p. 679).

[2] Forsyth, ii. 154. The good will of Lowe is evident here, but

Bertrand replied angrily that the Emperor would not accept favours from anybody, nor be indebted for anything to the caprice of any one, but that he claimed to be made acquainted with the restrictions imposed upon him. Sir Hudson answered: "I have not the pretension to bestow a favour on General Bonaparte, and still less the arrogance of subjecting him to any act of my caprice. He is under no restriction which my Government does not know, and which all the world may not know." Some time afterwards Lord Bathurst wrote to Sir Hudson Lowe that the Government, while approving of the Governor's having forwarded the presents to Napoleon under the circumstances, yet "in case of any present being hereafter forwarded to General Bonaparte to which emblems or titles of sovereignty are annexed, you are to consider that circumstance as altogether precluding its delivery, if they cannot be removed without prejudice to the present itself." It may be granted that this attitude is undignified and altogether unworthy of the British Government; but, as before remarked, the point to insist on is that Sir Hudson Lowe used his power to mitigate harshness and not to aggravate it. We come across another of O'Meara's misstatements in connexion with these very presents. He says that Captain Haviside, who brought them from China, "on having obtained permission to visit Longwood soon after his

the last sentence is ungraciously expressed, and it is not surprising that Bertrand resented it.

arrival, was ordered by the Governor to maintain a strict silence on the subject to all the French." [1] Years afterwards, on reading the passage in O'Meara's book, Captain Haviside spontaneously wrote to Sir Hudson Lowe, saying he trusted Sir Hudson would do him the honour to believe that he was not the author of this misrepresentation, that he had had every facility given him for visiting Longwood, and that he conversed some time with Count and Countess Bertrand on the subject of the presents. And yet the misrepresentation is repeated in the 1888 edition of O'Meara, no notice whatever being taken of Captain Haviside's contradiction! Soon after his arrival at St. Helena, Sir Hudson Lowe sent up some fowling-pieces to Longwood. This was resented as an insult, on the ground that the parts of the island where game could be shot were outside the precincts of Longwood; and yet at another time the servant Santini boasted that he supplied the table with the game he shot, when it was wished to make out that they were short of provisions! A writer in "The Leisure Hour" gives another instance:

"A wish on one occasion was expressed for a set of dining-tables. Immediately, as in every instance of the kind, no labour attainable on the island, and indeed no expense, was spared in order as expeditiously as possible to meet the requirements, and in a very

[1] "Voice from St. Helena," ii. 118.

short time a handsome mahogany set made its appearance at Longwood. When seeing it, one of the Emperor's most distinguished attendants gave orders for its removal, observing at the same time that it was not at all the thing the Emperor desired ; he wished for a plain deal table. Promptly, as before, was this wish also met, and a deal table accordingly was placed by direction in one of the dining-rooms at Longwood. On one occasion some visitors were conducted over several of the apartments, not excepting the dining-room referred to, with the deal table. The strangers, beholding the Emperor's humble dining-table, as intimated to them by their polite attendant with an expressive shrug, were at once overwhelmed with amazement and the deepest sympathy." [1]

On their return to England, these good people, with the best intentions, naturally gave this as an instance of the affronts and privations endured by the illustrious exile. Sir Hudson Lowe sent some excellent coffee to Longwood, thinking it would be an acceptable present. And so it was considered by Napoleon; but Count Montholon called it "an inexplicable idea of performing an act of politeness," and hesitated to convey the message about it to Napoleon, who, however, said, to his astonishment: "Cause the case to be carried to the pantry; good coffee is a precious

[1] "Leisure Hour," October 1st, 1870, "Recollections of St. Helena."

thing in this horrible place." Cipriani, the *maître-d'hôtel*, suspected that the coffee might be *poisoned*! Montholon adds: " In fact, the coffee was excellent." During February, 1821 (about two months before his death), Napoleon was attacked with constant sickness, and had great difficulty in keeping any food upon his stomach. Meat jelly made of veal was what he most easily retained, and when this was discovered some was immediately sent for his use from Plantation House, and a cook was also despatched by the Governor to Longwood who made excellent soup, of which Napoleon partook with much enjoyment. Count Montholon told Captain Lutyens (the orderly officer), " It was so good the d——d doctor would not let the Emperor eat much of it." We read also of the Governor sending books from his own library of the kind which Napoleon said he wanted, and he desired his secretary to make it known that he would attend to any further suggestions on the same subject. But perhaps enough has been said of the peculiar " brutality " of Sir Hudson Lowe. His generosity towards General Gourgaud has already been mentioned. Another striking instance is supplied by Mr. Henry, who says:

"When about to quit St. Helena, some of the foreigners were found to be considerably in debt to the shopkeepers in James Town, and one of the highest rank among them owed no less a sum than between nine hundred and a thousand pounds. Payment being delayed, legal measures were threatened, and all was consternation at Longwood. In this dilemma application was made to the Governor, who handsomely offered to guarantee payment of the debt, thus removing the principal difficulty in the way of their embarkation. I have heard that the amount was paid soon after their arrival in Europe, and I should expect nothing else from the high character of the distinguished debtor. This generous behaviour of the Governor, together with other acts of kindness to the exiles, after Napoleon's death, notwithstanding the abuse they had all publicly and privately showered upon his character, prove that Sir Hudson Lowe was a very different man from what he was represented by his enemies at the time, and what the world still believes him to be." [1]

Many years later one of the atrocious calumnies circulated against Sir Hudson Lowe was this : A paragraph appeared in a London paper stating (as a quotation from the " National ") that military executions were more frequent in Sicily then than they had been since the time that Sir Hudson Lowe held an appointment there. Sir Hudson Lowe wrote to the editor as follows:

" I feel impelled to address this note to you to desire it may be understood that I never was employed

[1] Henry, ii. 87.

as British Agent at the Neapolitan Court, and that I utterly deny the existence of a single circumstance of any description or import which can justify any person in presuming to couple my name with military trials or executions in Sicily or any other quarter of the globe."

And yet, after all, Sir Hudson Lowe's name had been connected with military executions in Calabria. But how? In an attempt to put a stop to them, as has already been mentioned, when he wrote to General Berthier thirty years earlier. Does not this well illustrate Sir Hudson's own remark that whatever kindness he "was guilty of" was turned against him?

His humanity was shown on a larger scale by a measure which has attracted little attention, but which links the name of Sir Hudson Lowe most honourably with the island of St. Helena. In 1818 he obtained the consent of the slave proprietors, not without some difficulty, to abolish slavery without receiving any compensation. It was resolved at a meeting of the chief proprietors "that from and after the 25th December next ensuing all children born of slaves shall be considered free." Thus the abolition was unattended with expense, and the mischief of sudden emancipation avoided. Sir Hudson Lowe's skill and management on this occasion were highly appreciated by the East India Company, who thus cleared all their possessions from this institution.[1] In reference to this

[1] See Appendix C.

measure at St. Helena, Sir Thomas Fowell Buxton made the following remarks in the House of Commons on May 15th, 1823, upon his motion for the abolition of slavery. After stating that the extinction of slavery which he declared to be his object was to be effected by ordaining that all negro children born after a certain day should be free, he thus continued :

" My opponents say that it will be attended with violence and convulsion. Then I put it to my opponent if he know where this noisy, turbulent, convulsive principle is at work? . . . The same [has occurred] at St. Helena. Public curiosity has recently been excited in an extraordinary degree. Books enough to fill a library have been written detailing the administration of Sir Hudson Lowe. Acts the most slight, anecdotes the most trivial, expressions the most unmeaning have been recorded with exact fidelity. Generations yet unborn shall know that on such a day in July Sir Hudson Lowe pronounced that the weather was warm, and that on such a day in the following December Bonaparte uttered a conjecture that it would rain in the course of the week. Nothing has escaped the researches of the historian. Nothing has been overlooked by the curiosity of the public. *Nothing?* Yes, one thing has never been noticed, namely, that Sir Hudson Lowe gave the death-blow to slavery at St. Helena." [1]

[1] " Parliamentary Debates," ix. 267.

Napoleon died on the evening of May 5th, 1821. On that day the Governor went early to Longwood, stayed there the whole day, and did not return until all was over. Mr. Henry gives an interesting account of what followed:

"The important event of the day was naturally the chief topic of conversation in the evening, as Sir Hudson took a hurried dinner, previous to writing his despatches; and, in bare justice to an ill-used man, I can testify that, notwithstanding the bitter passages between the great departed and himself, the Governor spoke of him in a feeling, respectful, and most proper manner. Major Gorrequer (the Military Secretary), Sir Hudson and myself, walked for a short time before the door of Plantation House, conversing on the character of the deceased. One of us remarked that he was the greatest enemy England ever had. 'Well, gentlemen,' said the Governor, 'he was England's greatest enemy, and mine too, but I forgive him everything. On the death of a great man like him, we should only feel deep concern and regret.'" [1]

[1] Henry, ii. 80. Lord Rosebery remarks upon this (p. 218): "On learning the event Lowe spoke a few manly and fitting words." This is, I believe, the only place where Lord Rosebery says anything good of Sir Hudson Lowe, and it is therefore pleasant to quote it. Even here, however, I am unable entirely to agree with him. I think Lowe's words would have been in rather better taste if he had said nothing on this occasion of his own personal feelings. M. de Viel-Castel, who is throughout favour-

On the death of Napoleon the whole importance of Sir Hudson Lowe's employment vanished. The unpopularity of having been charged with that employment alone awaited him.

able to Lowe, is also of this opinion (see "Revue des Deux Mondes," 1855, vol. vii. p. 334): "Ce peu de paroles, qui expriment avec si peu de tact et de convenance un sentiment en lui-même honnête et bon, peignent parfaitement Sir Hudson Lowe."

CHAPTER XI

LOWE AFTER ST. HELENA

Reception by the King and Government.—Effect of O'Meara's
"Voice."—Failure of legal proceedings.—Sir Hudson Lowe's
neglect to vindicate himself and its results.—Sir Hudson Lowe
in Ceylon.—The Duke of Wellington's defence.—Death and
conclusion.

SIR HUDSON LOWE left St. Helena at the end
of July. Before his arrival in England Lord
Bathurst had written a despatch conveying to him the
King's marked approbation of his conduct during the
whole period of his government at St. Helena. Sir
Hudson Lowe was presented to the King on November 14th; and, when he was about to kiss his Majesty's
hand, the King took hold of his and shook it heartily,
saying: " I congratulate you most sincerely upon your
return, after a trial the most arduous and exemplary
that perhaps any man ever had. I have felt for your
situation, and may appeal to Lord Bathurst how frequently I have talked to him about you." Soon afterwards he was appointed to the first vacant colonelcy
of a regiment (the 93rd Highlanders) that occurred
after his return to England.

But evil days were at hand. In July, 1822, came out O'Meara's " Voice from St. Helena," and the sensation it produced is well described by Sir Hudson Lowe himself: " Public curiosity flew with eagerness to the repast; nothing was wanting to satisfy the cravings of the most credulous, the most inquisitive, or the most malignant mind. The highest authorities were not spared; but *I* was destined to be the real victim, upon whom the public indignation was to fall." Lord Rosebery says of Lowe: " Had he not been selected for the delicate and invidious post of Governor of St. Helena during Napoleon's residence, he might have passed through and out of life with the same tranquil distinction as other officers of his service and standing."[1] With this sentence we may agree, if for the first clause we substitute the words: "Had it not been for O'Meara's book"; for without that the estimate of the King and Government would have been that of the public.

Upon the publication of the "Voice" Sir Hudson Lowe resolved to have recourse to the law for redress, and the result was an application to the Court of King's Bench for a criminal information against O'Meara. Much time was consumed in selecting the most libellous passages from the book. The difficulty of this task was great, owing to the peculiar art with which it was composed and the studied care taken to avoid any direct accusation in points where any living testimony could be referred to. Time was, however, of the last

[1] " Napoleon: the Last Phase," p. 66.

importance, although Sir Hudson was not aware of it. It was not until the latter end of Hilary Term, 1823—*i.e.*, towards the end of the second term after the publication of the libel—that a rule *nisi* was applied for, and then, when granting it, it was hinted by the Lord Chief Justice that the rule was likely to be discharged, simply on the technical ground that it was too late. His words were:

" The only difficulty the Court has felt is the lateness of the application. I take it to be a settled rule, when you move for a criminal information against a magistrate or justice of the peace, you must come in the first term, or so early in the second term that he may show cause against the rule in that second term. You should not come so late in the second term as to postpone the showing cause till the third term. That is the case where the application is against a magistrate or justice of the peace. I am not aware at this moment that the same rule has been laid down with regard to other persons, though in general the tardiness of the application operates strongly on the Court against the parties making it. Yet, in this particular case, Sir Hudson Lowe is an officer of the public; he is one of his Majesty's officers; so that the parties are changed."

The anticipation proved correct, for when O'Meara's counsel showed cause against the rule being made absolute, he urged the fatal objection that it was out of time, without attempting to enter into the merits, and this objection was upheld. It is certainly very strange that the eminent counsel [1] who advised Sir Hudson Lowe should not have informed him of this risk. Sir Hudson next consulted his legal advisers as to the expediency of indicting O'Meara, or of bringing an action for damages; but his counsel (Mr. Tindal) said with perfect truth that the proper legal remedy had been already resorted to for the vindication of his character. He had cleared himself from every charge upon his oath, and if O'Meara challenged the truth of his denials he might test them by prosecuting Sir Hudson Lowe for perjury. But to assume that a man's character is cleared in any way by the refusal of a libeller to go on to prosecute for perjury is a notion that would occur to no one but a lawyer. It leaves the game entirely in the libeller's hands. The objection to an indictment was that it would not put in issue the truth or falsehood of the accusations contained in the libel, for Lord Campbell's Act was not then in existence. As to a civil action, it would be useless to incur the risk of obtaining only small damages, which would in reality be a triumph for the defendant. In fact, Sir Hudson Lowe's legal remedy was gone owing to the fatal delay. There was only one course now to be pursued, and another fatal mistake was made in not pursuing it. Sir Hudson Lowe should at once have vindicated his

[1] Copley, afterwards Lord Lyndhurst, and Tindal, afterwards Chief Justice of the Common Pleas.

character by the publication of a complete account of his governorship, for which he had the amplest materials, and the result could not have failed to redound to his public credit. Lord Bathurst, who was always his friend, strongly urged Sir Hudson Lowe to take this obvious course, and offered to place all the state documents at his disposal.[1] His continued silence could not fail to impress the public unfavourably. However innocent a man may be, he cannot allow the foulest charges to be brought against him and expect no one will believe them. In Jupiter or Saturn things may be arranged differently, but here the world judges, rightly or wrongly, that a man who does nothing to vindicate his character, when it has been publicly aspersed, does not do so because he cannot do so; and in ninety-nine cases out of a hundred the world's judgement is correct. But Sir Hudson Lowe's happened to be the hundredth case, and it cannot be denied that his failure to do what his position demanded brought on himself a penalty which he kept on suffering to the end of his life, and from which his memory still suffers. We cannot be surprised that Sir Hudson Lowe's enemies made the most of his unaccountable silence.

[1] It has been said that Lord Bathurst did not approve of any publication by Sir Hudson Lowe. What Lord Bathurst disapproved of was Sir Hudson Lowe's returning from Ceylon in 1828 in order to defend himself. He had written (November 28th, 1823) to Lowe saying that he owed it to himself to draw up a full and complete vindication of his administration at St. Helena after all that had been said against him.

It is therefore most material to consider why he did not follow the advice of Lord Bathurst and the rest of his friends. A man may, it is true, despise the opinion of the world and take no heed of calumny, either because he has a contempt for his fellow-creatures or from a motive of religion. But Sir Hudson Lowe was neither a cynic nor a saint. He lived for the world, and promotion in his profession naturally depended to a large extent on his retaining the good opinion of the world. To complain of calumnies, and yet to neglect the only steps by which they can be abated, shows a certain amount of wrong-headedness, for which it is difficult to account completely. However, some of the reasons by which the ex-Governor was actuated in refusing to make an appeal to public opinion may be conjectured. The scruples that stood in his way are all those of a high-minded man, but they do more honour to his heart than to his head. First, then, Sir Hudson Lowe despised his enemies, more especially O'Meara. That individual was certainly worthy of all the contempt which the ex-Governor felt for him ; but then the public did not know what Sir Hudson knew, and it is simply a blunder to despise an adversary who assumes to bring forward *facts* and not merely his own *opinions*. Such alleged facts, by whomsoever stated, must be shown to be untrue. The consciousness of having honourably discharged a difficult duty does not, as Mr. Forsyth well remarks, " inspire enthusiasm in others, or cause friends to cluster round the object

of calumny and reproach." Secondly, Sir Hudson
Lowe thought that, as his conduct had been heartily
approved by the King and Government, it was rather
for the latter than for himself to undertake his defence.
But surely this was expecting too much. A body of
men like a Government can never act with the generosity of an individual. They have seldom time or in-
clination to vindicate the character of a servant, unless
their own stability is so much bound up with that
servant as to make his defence practically the same as
their own. This was not the case here. It would not be
too much to say that the opposite of this was the case.
While a Government cannot be as generous as an
individual, it can, and sometimes does, like any other
body of men, act with a meanness of which most
individuals would be ashamed, and at this time the
Government by sacrificing Sir Hudson Lowe strengthened their own position, and to a large extent took
the wind from the sails of the Opposition. When they
were attacked for their ill-treatment of Napoleon they
could tacitly transfer the odium of it to Sir Hudson
Lowe, for Mr. Forsyth puts it too mildly when he says:
" The Government ought to have aided Sir Hudson
Lowe more heartily and effectually than they did." In
the third place, and probably this weighed most of all
with the chivalrous nature of Sir Hudson, who was in-
tensely loyal to his King and country, he clearly per-
ceived that he could not thoroughly defend himself
without disclosing the shabby manner in which he had

been treated by the Government during his term of office at St. Helena. He knew that O'Meara's correspondence had been encouraged by Cabinet Ministers, and that intrigues behind his back had, to say the least, not been discouraged. But I have already dealt with this topic, and need not repeat my words. It is evident that Sir Hudson Lowe acutely felt the delicacy of his position. But surely all his scruples should have been set at rest by the strongly urged advice of Lord Bathurst to publish—Lord Bathurst, who was himself one of the principal members of the Cabinet, and who knew more about St. Helena than all the rest.

As a matter of fact, after the return of Sir Hudson Lowe nothing was ever done for him by the Government at all adequate to his merits. He certainly received from them plenty of empty praise, but *probitas laudatur et alget* ("honesty is praised and—left out in the cold"), for, while those who had served under him at St. Helena were promoted on *his* recommendation, nothing was done for himself. Before he ever went to St. Helena he had been formally assured that Lord Liverpool had said that, if he went, "it should not stop there."[1] Sir Hudson Lowe was then advised by a friend of some experience to stipulate for a pension before he went out, but he did not follow the suggestion. He felt too confident of the principles upon which he should discharge the duty entrusted to him not to be assured that recompense must follow. The

[1] See above, p. 69.

employment was therefore accepted without any endeavour on his part to establish any condition.[1] Colonel Wilks, his predecessor at St. Helena, was in receipt of a pension of £1,500. Sir Hudson Lowe had no pension given to him. It is said that Lord Liverpool was prejudiced against him. The calumnies of O'Meara may indeed have had this effect. The writer of Sir Hudson Lowe's life in the "Dictionary of National Biography" says: "The amount of his salary (£12,000 a year) was specially fixed, and no stipulation was made as to pension, which explains the fact, upon which his enemies remarked, that he was not afterwards considered eligible for a pension." But surely this must be an error, or Sir Hudson Lowe would not so persistently have urged his claim to a pension, and we never find that the obvious reply that he was not eligible for one was made, but only that if it was submitted to the House of Commons they would not grant it. The Government no doubt must have felt that they had not treated Sir Hudson Lowe fairly, and when the storm burst upon his head they were not inclined to help him, for the vigorous lines of Dryden are ever true:

> Forgiveness to the injured doth belong,
> But they ne'er pardon who have done the wrong.

Another disadvantage under which Sir Hudson Lowe laboured was that he knew so few people in England

[1] See Memoir, "United Service Magazine," June, 1844, p. 290.

at the time. All his active military life, previous to his departure for St. Helena, had been spent in Continental service, and most of the friends he then made were now dead. Lord Bathurst offered him in 1824 the government of the island of Antigua (a post ridiculously below his merits), but family reasons prevented him from accepting it. He was in the following year appointed to the command of the forces in Ceylon with a prospect, if not a promise, of the reversion of the governorship. As the "Eastern Question" was even then one of importance, he resolved to go out by the overland route. Being a man of great physical as well as moral courage, he disregarded the advice of his friends and determined to pass through Paris. While Sir Hudson was approaching Paris in his carriage, young Las Cases was found wounded near a spot by which Sir Hudson passed, and it was reported that an attempt had been made by Sir Hudson Lowe to assassinate him! The "Times" commented upon the rumour as follows:

"Our readers will see in our French letter a curious result drawn from the supposed attempt to assassinate young Las Cases. Sir Hudson Lowe, lately at Paris, and now on his way home,[1] is charged with that attempt. We expected that such would be the case; and it was by mere chance that we did not make an observation

[1] This was a mistake. He was on his way to Ceylon at this time.

to that effect when we inserted the paragraph with the rumour of the assassination. We have not the least doubt but that the whole is a plot against Sir Hudson. Some people will say that he might as well have kept away from Paris, unless he had urgent business there; others, that he did right to show himself, in the consciousness of an innocent heart and the pride of having done his duty. We shall not decide upon this point. We thought that the journey to Paris exposed Sir Hudson to some risk, without knowing of what kind the risk might be. The moment we heard the assassination story, we saw in what way the Bonapartists were going to work." [1]

The hoax was rather too palpable, and nothing more was heard of it.

On reaching Vienna Sir Hudson Lowe learnt that the Emperor Alexander had sent instructions to his Minister at Vienna not only to furnish him with the necessary passports for travelling through any part of the Russian dominions, but had also given directions that he should be received with the highest military honours wherever he passed. He hoped to have met the Emperor in the south of Russia, but the news of the Emperor's death caused Sir Hudson to alter his route and proceed across the Balkans to Constantinople, his object being to see as much as he could of Turkey and form his own opinion of its defences. Here he was

[1] "Times," November 19th, 1825.

welcomed by Sir Stratford Canning, who had just arrived as Ambassador, and who facilitated his journey in
every way. At Smyrna another danger awaited him.
While he was dining on board H.M.S. *Cambrian* with
Captain Hamilton, the secretary of the French Consul
proceeded to Sir Hudson Lowe's lodgings with the
avowed intention of assassinating him. Not finding
him in, this worthy destroyed some of Sir Hudson's
property, and prepared to lie in wait for his return,
calling upon a friend to be "witness of the revenge he
was about to take on the murderer and poisoner of
Napoleon." From doing this, however, he was prevented, and the matter becoming known, the French
Consul dismissed the man from his employment. Sir
Hudson Lowe, on receiving an assurance that he
should be no further molested, and learning that his
would-be assailant had a large family dependent upon
him for support, wrote that "he had no desire to take
any further steps in the affair, or to stand in the way
of any act of lenity or consideration which the French
Consul himself might think fit to show towards him."[1]
Such was the vindictive spirit exhibited by the "murderer and poisoner" of Napoleon.

We have already seen that Sir Hudson Lowe returned from Ceylon to England in 1828 in order to
vindicate his character. On his way home he called
in at St. Helena. He found Longwood already con-
verted to the basest uses, and Lord Rosebery leaves

[1] From an unpublished letter.

us to imagine what Lowe's feelings may have been at beholding this scene of desolation and disgrace. Whatever they may have been, he was not responsible for the condition of Napoleon's former habitation, and we know that as a fact he was most cordially welcomed by the inhabitants, who remembered the justice and kindness of his rule as civil Governor.[1] When he re-embarked after three days' stay, during which a public entertainment was given him by the inhabitants and another by the military, he was attended to the waterside and cheered by those who had welcomed him as their guest. This tribute, says Mr. Forsyth,[2] was spontaneous, and as such was deeply felt by the man who had so long been the object of unmerited odium. It was also the more valuable as offered in the place where his character was best known and his conduct most fully understood.

Again ill-luck followed him. The governorship of Ceylon fell vacant near the end of 1830, a very short time after Earl Grey had become Prime Minister. All hope of public employment was now over for the time, for, as Mr. Forsyth remarks, "neither Earl Grey nor his colleagues could be expected to sympathize much with the former guardian of Napoleon's person, of whom it had been so long the fashion of their party to speak as the inhuman jailer of an injured prisoner."

Sir Hudson Lowe's military command in Ceylon terminated with his promotion to the rank of Lieu-

[1] See Appendix C.   [2] Forsyth, iii. 330.

tenant-General in 1830[1] (in St. Helena he held this only as a local rank), and after his return to England in 1831 he was incessantly occupied in petitioning—one might almost say pestering—the Government for some office in recognition of his services, not merely on account of his private means, which had become much reduced, but also as some answer to the calumnies so industriously circulated against him. But calumny and uncontradicted lies had at last done their natural work. Some of the mud so copiously thrown had stuck, and stuck effectually. In a memorial drawn up in 1843 Sir Hudson Lowe writes, after alluding to the state of inactivity in which he had been kept for twelve years:

" The government of the island of Ceylon had thrice fallen vacant, and the chief authority in the Ionian Islands (where my local services at their liberation and in the discharge of *civil* and military duties subsequently had contributed to form a strong claim for re-employment) four times, during the period of which I have been speaking. Vacancies had also arisen in other stations. But on none of these occasions were either my local or general services, or any claim arising from past disappointment, taken into that consideration which I should have hoped might have been deemed to be their due."

[1] For two opinions of Sir Hudson Lowe in Ceylon see Appendix B.

But it was not all gloom. Even the malice of his foes gave occasion to the championship of friends who were above the influence of party spirit. In 1833 Lord Teynham made an attack on Sir Hudson Lowe in the House of Lords. Speaking of the government of Ireland, he said, in reference to a proposal to entrust special powers to the Lord-Lieutenant (the Marquis of Normanby): "Now suppose the noble Marquis were to be succeeded in the government of Ireland by a Sir Hudson Lowe." Here he was called to order, and when he had sat down the Duke of Wellington rose, and, asking what the noble Lord meant, said: "I have the honour to know Sir Hudson Lowe, and I will say, in this House or elsewhere, wherever it may be, that there is not in the army a more respectable officer than Sir Hudson Lowe, nor has his Majesty a more faithful subject." A day or two afterwards Lord Teynham made an abject apology, and in reply to a letter of thanks from Sir Hudson Lowe to the Duke for his prompt and generous defence, the latter wrote as follows:

"STRATHFIELDSAYE, *Feb.* 21, 1833.

"MY DEAR GENERAL,

"I have received your letter of the 20th. I assure you that I considered that I did no more than my duty upon the occasion to which you refer in repelling a very gross and marked insinuation against an officer, in his absence, for whom I entertained the highest respect and regard. The discusssion ended in a way that must be highly satisfactory to all your friends.

" Ever, my dear General, yours most faithfully,

" WELLINGTON.

" Lieut.-General Sir Hudson Lowe."

In 1842 Sir Hudson Lowe was much gratified by his transfer to the colonelcy of his old regiment, the 50th, the regiment in which he had first received a commission.[1] In the same year the King of Prussia advanced him to the First Class of the Red Eagle of Prussia, notified in a flattering letter from Baron von Bülow, who recalled his " signal services to the common cause in the glorious campaigns of 1813-14."[2] He was also made a G.C.M.G., an order which at that time was confined to those who had rendered service in connexion with Malta or the Ionian Islands.

It is pleasing to record, on the authority of his eldest son, that in spite of all his troubles Sir Hudson Lowe was never depressed. " This frame of mind appeared to be one of which he was always incapable. Up to his final seizure with paralysis he had always abundant animal spirits. To say that he retained his activity of mind and body and his industry to the last would be inappropriate, as they may be rather considered as having been too great for his strength."[3] Most men

---

[1] See Appendix C.

[2] " Dictionary of National Biography," vol. xxxiv. p. 193.

[3] Memoir, " United Service Magazine," June, 1844, p. 294.

would have become embittered or morose under the long persecution of which Sir Hudson Lowe was the victim. He died on the 10th of January, 1844, in comparative poverty. His body lies, together with that of Lady Lowe, in the crypt of St. Mark's Church, North Audley Street. In the porch is a tablet to their memory. Sir Robert Peel recommended Miss Lowe, his unmarried daughter, to the Queen for a small pension which at the time was at his disposal, "in recognition of the services of her father." This lady still survives to cherish the memory of a father whose domestic virtues have never been questioned by his bitterest assailants.

Such, then, was the career of Sir Hudson Lowe, a man of unstained honour, of undaunted courage, of unflinching resolution. He was as much devoted to duty as the Duke of Wellington. With the latter "the path of duty was the way to glory." With Sir Hudson Lowe this was not the case; but, after all, there may be better things than "glory."

> For this, thy track, across the fretful foam
> Of vehement actions without scope or term,
> Call'd history, keeps a splendour; due to wit,
> Which saw one clue to life, and follow'd it.

The defects of Lowe's character are clear enough. I have made no effort, and it would be useless, to try to conceal them. He was wanting in breadth of view in insisting too much on the letter of his instructions, he was wanting in tact in some of his dealings with the Emperor, and in the position he occupied such de-

fects were of great importance; but he was not wanting
in delicacy, generosity, and self-control. All his faults
were due to want of imagination, not to want of heart.
Count Balmain, who was one of the shrewdest ob-
servers on the island, said of him : " The Governor is
not a tyrant, but he is difficult to get on with." In the
eyes of the admirers of Napoleon, Sir Hudson Lowe
has the supreme fault of not being fascinated by their
idol—of treating him, in fact, almost as if he were of
the same clay as himself. By nature Lowe was irritable
and suspicious. The former quality was certainly never
exhibited in the presence of Napoleon, though perhaps before his subordinates or the ridiculous Montchenu he may occasionally have shown temper. The
latter quality was to his own Government a recommendation in the nervous and excited state of the
public mind of Europe. He was, in fact, intended to
err, if at all, on the side of suspicion. His career shows
—but there was no need to show it—the inadequacy
of the copy-book view of life. *Magna est veritas et
praevalebit*, we read. Perhaps so, if the future tense
may be extended into another existence. Meantime
it is often truer to say *Magnum est mendacium et prae-
valuit*, if the lying is sufficiently systematic and persistent. In course of time a venerable lie may come to
earn the prescription that should be due only to truth.
We find, again, that faults of manner and method are
far more severely punished in this world than real de-
pravity. A man may break all the ten commandments

if he has sufficient natural force to do so on a large scale, not merely with impunity, but with the certainty of becoming the object of extensive admiration.

Sir Hudson Lowe has been the most calumniated man of the last—perhaps of any—century. He has been charged with giving way to ungovernable bursts of temper; Napoleon complained that he could not make him lose his temper. He has been charged with want of courtesy; all Napoleon could say against him was that on one occasion, after being assailed with a torrent of abuse, he actually forgot himself so far as to retire rather abruptly and without the customary bow! He has been charged with want of delicacy; if he had been less delicate he would have vindicated himself with more success. He has been charged with harshness and brutality in the discharge of his duty; the only official hint of disapproval that he ever received from the Government was on account of his leniency. The British Government showed, no doubt, some want of generosity in their treatment of Napoleon. They were not quite without excuse. But their conduct towards him was generosity itself compared with their conduct towards their own servant. Here they were without excuse.

It is to the honour of England that the truth of this miserable affair should be known, and the more widely it is known the more will it become recognized that Englishmen have no cause to be ashamed of the conduct of Sir Hudson Lowe at St. Helena.

APPENDIX A

THE DUKE OF WELLINGTON AND SIR HUDSON
LOWE

See pages 67, 68, 243, above.

THE opinion of the Duke of Wellington always
carries very great weight with Englishmen. It
is, therefore, a matter of importance to know what
opinion he has expressed about Sir Hudson Lowe.

We have seen above that the statement in the
"American Cyclopaedia" that Sir Hudson Lowe had
some feeling of resentment against the Duke, and that
the charge of Napoleon's person was conferred upon
him to "soothe his feelings," rests upon an entire mis-
apprehension of the circumstances. The statement,
on the other hand, that Sir Hudson was in any sense
the Duke's "tool" at St. Helena is equally erroneous.
We need not deal with these aspects of the case any
further.

We have also seen that when Sir Hudson Lowe
was attacked in the House of Lords, in 1833, the
Duke defended him, and in reply to the thanks of
Sir Hudson wrote the letter given on p. 243, which I
make no apology for repeating here:

"STRATHFIELDSAYE, *Feb.* 21, 1833.

" MY DEAR GENERAL,

"I have received your letter of the 20th. I assure you that I considered that I did no more than my duty upon the occasion to which you refer in repelling a very gross and marked insinuation against an officer, in his absence, for whom I entertained the highest respect and regard. The discussion ended in a way that must be highly satisfactory to all your friends.

" Ever, my dear General, yours most faithfully,

"WELLINGTON.

" Lieut.-General Sir Hudson Lowe."

Some have considered that this letter was merely a polite acknowledgement on the Duke's part. But it is well known that the Duke never did write mere letters of compliment, and we must therefore take it that he meant what he said.

Lord Rosebery quotes the Duke of Wellington as follows: "Sir Hudson Lowe was a very bad choice; he was a man wanting in education and judgement. He was a stupid man, he knew nothing at all of the world, and like all men who know nothing of the world, he was suspicious and jealous." [1] The reader would naturally suppose that the words quoted were uttered by the Duke at one and the same time without any qualification; but, as a fact, they are taken from two utterances with a long interval of time between, and with all that is favourable to Lowe suppressed. They are to be found in Lord Stanhope's

---

[1] " Napoleon: the Last Phase," p. 68.

" Notes of Conversations with the Duke of Wellington,"
as follows :

"*Oct.* 31*st*, 1835.—The Duke, in answer to my inquiries, said that he thought the treatment of Napoleon
at St. Helena gave no substantial ground of complaint,
but that Sir H. Lowe was a very bad choice. He was
a man wanting education and judgement."

"*Dec.* 21*st*, 1848.—I told the Duke that I had lately
read some proofs of the forthcoming book, compiled
from the papers of Sir Hudson Lowe at St. Helena. The
Duke said he was confident they would prove to be false,
the principal charges flung out against Sir Hudson.
I agreed to this, and observed that I supposed the
Duke had scarcely known Sir Hudson Lowe personally.
' Yes, I did ; I knew him very well. He was a stupid
man.' I conceive, said I, that he had a bad irritable
temper, and in that point was ill-qualified for his post.
' He was not an ill-natured man. But he knew nothing
at all of the world, and like all men who know nothing
of the world, he was suspicious and jealous.' "

There is another remark referring to Lowe which
Lord Rosebery has not given:

"*Oct.* 19*th*, 1837.—Is it true, Sir, that at the Congress
of Aix-la-Chapelle, Austria remonstrated on our treatment of Napoleon as severe ? ' Nothing of the kind
happened. Without being any great admirer of Sir
Hudson Lowe, I must say that I think he has been
shamefully used about this business—shamefully.' "

It may be said that the Duke of Wellington would
hardly have thus spoken of a man for whom he " enter-

tained the highest respect and regard," and that therefore the language of the letter must be discounted *pro
tanto* by the language of the conversation. It cannot
be denied that there is a certain inconsistency between
the two which cannot be entirely accounted for by the
difference between writing and speaking. However, I
do not attempt to reconcile them. Let them stand
side by side. I will only remark that to pick out the
unfavourable parts from two quotations and put them
together as one is as misleading and unfair as to quote
incorrectly.

APPENDIX B

SIR HUDSON LOWE IN CEYLON

See pages 238, 241, 242, above.

THERE are two notices of Sir Hudson Lowe in Ceylon which are interesting as giving a very different view of his character from that usually presented. The first is from the " Memoirs of a Highland Lady," which is the autobiography of Elizabeth Grant of Rothiemurchus, afterwards Mrs. Smith of Baltiboys, edited by Lady Strachey, pp. 459, 460:

" I was taken to dinner by a grave, particularly gentlemanly man in a general's uniform, whose conversation was as agreeable as his manners.[1] He had been over half the world, knew all celebrities, and contrived, without display, to say a great deal one was willing to hear. About the middle of dinner the Governor called out, 'Sir Hudson Lowe, a glass of wine with you '—people did such barbarities then— to which my companion bowed assent. Years before, with our Whig principles and prejudice, we had cultivated in our Highland retirement a horror of the great Napoleon's gaoler. The cry of party, the feeling for

[1] Lord Rosebery says (p. 66) of Sir Hudson Lowe: "We are afraid we must add that he was not what we should call, in the best sense, a gentleman." *Utri creditis, Quirites?*

the prisoner, the book of Surgeon O'Meara, the ' Voice from St. Helena,' had all worked my woman's heart to such a pitch of indignation, that this maligned name was an offence. We were to hold the owner in abhorrence, speak to him, never! look at him, sit in the same room with him, never! None were louder than I, more vehement; yet here I was beside my bugbear and perfectly satisfied with the position. It was a good lesson. He had been sent to Ceylon because he was so miserable at home. People, judging him as we had done, tabooed him remorselessly. He was so truly sent to Coventry that he once thanked Colonel Pennington in a coffee-house for the common civility of handing him a newspaper, saying that any civility was now so new to him he must be excused for gratefully acknowledging it. The opinion of less partial times has judged more fairly of Sir Hudson, his captive, and the surgeon. Timidity and anxiety made Sir Hudson unnecessarily vexatious, Bonaparte was not in a mood to be placable, and Mr. O'Meara wanted money and notoriety, which he gained at no expense."

The second notice is from " Fifty Years in Ceylon," by Major Thomas Skinner, C.M.G. From the account here given it would seem that Sir Hudson Lowe's nerve had weakened, probably from the treatment he had received. The passage is as follows (pp. 74, 75):

" I had not held my appointment very long before Sir Hudson Lowe arrived as second in command, and after some persuasion assumed the duties of Commandant of Colombo. He had not held any command of the kind for some time. A general impression prevailed that Sir Hudson Lowe was a surly, austere man, but never was a character more maligned; a more kind, I may say tender-hearted man, I never met with. For a military commander it almost amounted to a fault, for it was with extreme difficulty we could get him to notice irregularities, or to punish breaches of discipline. If I had not had the support and co-operation of his A.D.C., Oliver De Lancy, the discipline of the garrison would soon have fallen off under his command.

" He was terribly undecided, and I have often wondered how his wavering mind could have carried him so far through the service, or enabled him to perform those delicate duties which were imposed upon him. I retained until very lately a striking proof of this characteristic. He was involved in a correspondence with the Government on an important question connected with the duties of his command. On my waiting on him one morning, he desired me to sit down and write a letter from his dictation. He paced up and down a long room, the whole width of his house, and in three hours finished and corrected his composition. I read it to him, and he desired me to take it home, copy it, and bring it to him for his signature. I obeyed his orders, but was far from obtaining his signature. I had to sit down again ' to make a few verbal alterations,' and this was repeated until I had seven copies of the letter; the one to which he finally attached his signature proved to be a very slight deviation from the original draft.

" I never could understand why none of Sir Hudson Lowe's works were ever published, for he had undoubtedly several on hand, and a very large quantity of MS. ready for the press. Two or three amanuenses were continually engaged by him, and many reams of foolscap paper were filled, and so arranged in his private room as to indicate that there were at least three subjects to which his attention at the time was devoted. No circumstances could have been more favourable to quiet reflection than those of his life. He was very hospitable and generous; kept an excellent table and first-rate cellar."

APPENDIX C

SIR HUDSON LOWE AS A CIVIL GOVERNOR

See pages 121, 217, 225, 241, 244, above.

From the "Times," November 22nd, 1842.

"WE have much pleasure in recording the appointment of Lieut.-General Sir Hudson Lowe to the Colonelcy of the 50th Regiment. There is no officer of Sir Hudson's rank and services in the army who has been more unworthily used. For performing a duty of the most difficult and ungracious description with the most zealous fidelity, he received, it is true, numerous and highly complimentary letters from the Government, acknowledging, as they were bound to do, the important services he had rendered; whilst he became a mark of public obloquy of the most inveterate description, because he had never permitted himself to be provoked into the slightest violation of that duty. His position was certainly a most embarrassing one, but the chief cause of his unpopularity with his capricious captive was the equanimity of his temper, and the coolness and imperturbability with which he carried the minutest instructions of his employers into effect. Napoleon's expression, 'If I could but make that man bang the door!' affords a sufficient key to the difficulty of the task he had to

S

perform. Like a true soldier he could not be influenced by either taunts or cajolery, and for this Napoleon hated him most inveterately, and libelled him on every possible opportunity. His Whig friends at home, in and out of Parliament, did the same; until poor Sir Hudson became 'the best abused man' in Europe; until the very people who had calumniated him had repeated their allegations so frequently without contradiction, that they began half to believe that they were true. Meanwhile, Whig lampoons and Jacobin newspapers assailed him, almost for years, with daily torrents of abuse. Yet, with the means of replying to those calumnies in the most satisfactory manner, and of putting them down at once and for ever, he has preserved a dignified silence, and has verified the correctness of Southey's lines:

> Evil and good report we soon live down
> If undeserved.

We repeat then our gratification that the present Government has at length evinced the disposition to repair, in some degree, the injustice of which Sir Hudson Lowe has been the victim."

From the " Times," November 26th, 1842.

" *To the Editor of the Times.*

" SIR,

"Every one who has had the honour of knowing Sir Hudson Lowe during the time he was Governor of St. Helena, and had charge of Napoleon Bonaparte, must feel gratified at your defence of his public character and conduct in your paper of the 22d inst. I say all must rejoice, whether naval, military, or inhabitants, of all which classes there are many in this country willing to bear testimony to his high and honourable character, and his humane consideration for the poor and distressed, which induced him not only to expend large sums in charity (not always known at the time), but to afford relief in very many instances to the families of those of a higher class, who in sickness stood in need of such things as were difficult to be obtained in a place where living was expensive and fresh provisions sometimes scarce. Sir Hudson Lowe ever maintained a character during the time he was on the island for strict impartiality and justice, coupled with the utmost consideration and kindness for all beneath his rule; his hospitality was unbounded (without due regard to his private fortune), and upon this point all the classes I have enumerated would, I am sure, cheerfully bear testimony. To show the high sense the servants of the East India Company and the inhabitants entertained of his conduct towards them during the time he was Governor, I will only mention that, on his return to the island, on his homeward-bound voyage from Ceylon, where he had been in a military capacity, he was welcomed with every demonstration of joy; he was invited by all classes to a public entertainment, and he was afterwards entertained at the military mess; and upon leaving for his ship at night, he was followed to the landing-place by a large concourse of his friends, who were anxious to manifest their respect and gratitude towards him by every means in their power; and had he touched a second time at the island, as was expected, his reception would have been the same.

"I may, I trust, be excused mentioning another circumstance, which shows the high respect the inhabitants entertained for him at an early stage of his government, when he called them together at the Castle, and after setting forth in an admirable address his views on the subject of slavery, but doing them justice in acknowledging the mild and equitable treatment slaves experienced on the island, he proposed that the proprietors should, by some act of their own, set an example towards abolishing this revolting system. The inhabitants who were slave proprietors immediately came to the resolution, 'That after Christmas-day in that year (1818) all children born of slave parents should be declared free'—a resolution carefully kept and observed, so that after the present generation of slaves had died off, slavery would have ceased to exist, even had the East India Company not thought fit to emancipate them some years afterwards. I do not mean to reflect on the inhabitants, but I feel assured Sir Hudson Lowe was the only person who had influence enough to induce them to adopt this resolution, so highly creditable to them. I will only add, that the inhabitants generally remember with the liveliest feelings of affection the charities and benevolence of Lady Lowe.

"I am, Sir, your obedient Servant,

"An Old Inhabitant of St. Helena.

"*November 24th.*"

APPENDIX D

THERE is in existence a book entitled "Mémorial de Sir Hudson Lowe relatif à la captivité de Napoléon à Sainte-Hélène," which purports to be an autobiography of Sir Hudson Lowe. The copy I have seen is in one volume, 12mo, pp. 396, published at Brussels, 1830; but it is referred to in works of reference as published at Paris, in two volumes, 1830. It has even been translated into German. To any one who is even slightly acquainted with the subject the book is an obvious and impudent forgery. Holzhausen, in his "Napoleon's Tod," speaks of it (p. 73 n.) as "eine offenbare Fälschung, die von den allergröbsten Fehlern wimmelt." It contains a most forbidding, but quite imaginary, portrait of Lowe, the same, indeed, as appears in Prof. Sloane's "Life of Napoleon" (where one is surprised to see it). Sir Hudson Lowe's portrait was only once taken—a pencil drawing by Wyvill, in 1832, as stated in the Preface. It is reproduced here, and an engraving from it is prefixed to Forsyth's "History of the Captivity of Napoleon."

The animus that breathes through this book is sufficiently indicated by the following sentence in the anonymous editor's preface:

" Si nous eussions pensé un seul instant que les documents et les notes que nous publions pussent faire trouver grâce à Sir Hudson Lowe, devant un seul de nos compatriotes; s'il nous eût été possible de supposer que sa conduite envers son noble prisonnier parût un peu moins déshonorante, un peu moins hideuse, nous nous serions bien gardés de jeter dans la nation une publication aussi immorale."

The authorship is uncertain. It has been attributed to the younger Las Cases, among others, but the point is of no importance. The book does not profess to be a translation from the English, as one might expect; indeed, the opening words of the preface—" Ces notes que le gouverneur de Sainte-Hélène à tracées à la hâte et qui sont redigées sans ordre et sans plan, nous les transmettons au lecteur, telles que Sir Hudson Lowe les a écrites "—seem to imply that Sir Hudson Lowe wrote it in French. This in itself would be in the highest degree improbable, for, although he was well acquainted with French, it would be to his own countrymen that he would appeal, not to foreigners.

What is surprising is that any one should have thought it worth while to concoct such a book, though it may seem presumptuous to set limits to the excesses of partisan hatred. What is still more surprising is that it has been accepted as genuine in such well-known and usually reliable works of reference as Brockhaus' " Konversations-Lexikon," Meyer's " Kon-versations-Lexikon," and the " American Cyclopaedia." Madame de Montholon also, in her " Souvenirs de Sainte-Hélène," speaks of the " curieux mémoires " of Sir Hudson Lowe. In view of these facts it may be as well to state shortly the decisive reasons for regarding this book as a forgery—a book which otherwise might be left undisturbed in dishonourable obscurity.

1. The mistakes in matters of fact are innumerable. For instance, the date and place of Lowe's birth are wrongly given; his father is stated to have been an ironmonger in Lombard Street; Lowe is said to have gone to Calcutta, never to have smelt powder, to have demanded his recall from St. Helena, to have been refused an interview with George IV. after his return, etc., etc.

2. The whole attitude here depicted is contrary to the attitude really taken up by Sir Hudson Lowe. He is here made to admit the charges of brutality made against him, and to defend himself by saying that he was only obeying his instructions. In reality Sir Hudson Lowe always considered that he had claims upon the Government for good service rendered, not that he had done anything that needed apology.

3. It is well known that Sir Hudson Lowe, contrary to the advice of his best friends and of members of the Government, never published any vindication of himself, which he had ample materials for doing. He thought, no doubt erroneously, that it was the duty of the Government who had approved his administration to undertake his defence when it became necessary.

CHRONOLOGICAL TABLE

1815. July 15. Surrender of Napoleon to Captain Maitland on board the *Bellerophon*.

Aug. 2. Convention between the Powers with reference to the foreign Commissioners.

,, 7. Transhipment of Napoleon and his suite to the *Northumberland*, off Berry Head.

Oct. 15. Arrival in St. Helena of Rear-Admiral Sir George Cockburn on board the *Northumberland*, conveying Napoleon and his suite, including the surgeon, O'Meara.

Dec. 10. Removal of Napoleon from The Briars to Longwood.

1816. April 14. Arrival of Sir Hudson Lowe and suite on board the *Phaeton*.

,, 16. *First* interview between Napoleon and Sir Hudson Lowe.

,, 30. *Second* interview.

May 17. *Third* interview.

June 17. Arrival of Rear-Admiral Sir Pulteney Malcolm on board the *Newcastle* frigate, to succeed Sir George Cockburn in command of the naval station at St. Helena; also of the three foreign Commissioners.

July 17. *Fourth* interview.

Aug. 18. *Fifth* and last interview.

,, 23. Remonstrance of Montholon.

Oct. 9. The "new regulations."

265

1816. Dec. 30. Departure of Las Cases and his son.
1817. June 29. Arrival of Rear-Admiral Plampin to succeed
Sir Pulteney Malcolm.
1818. Mar. 14. Departure of General Gourgaud.
July 11. Departure of Baron Stürmer (Austrian
Commissioner).
Aug. 2. Departure of O'Meara.
1819. Sep. 20. Arrival of Dr. Antommarchi.
1820. May 3. Departure of Count Balmain (Russian
Commissioner).
July. Arrival of Rear-Admiral Lambert to succeed
Rear-Admiral Plampin.
1821. May 5. Death of Napoleon.
„ 9. Funeral of Napoleon.
„ 27. Departure of the French attendants.[1]
July 25. Departure of Sir Hudson Lowe and suite.

[1] According to Forsyth. Mr. Henry, who accompanied them, gives the date of departure as May 21st, while Count Montholon says May 30th.

BIBLIOGRAPHY

(The following list does not claim to be exhaustive)

ORIGINAL SOURCES

1. "Letters written on board the *Northumberland* and at St. Helena, on Napoleon and his Suite." By William Warden. London, 1816. 8vo.

2. "An Appeal to the British Nation on the Treatment experienced by Napoleon Bonaparte in the Island of St. Helena." By M. Santine, Huissier du cabinet de l'Empereur. London, 1816. 8vo. [This pamphlet was really by Colonel Maceroni.]

3. "Letters from the Cape of Good Hope, in reply to Mr. Warden." 1817. 8vo. [Chiefly from Napoleon's dictation.]

4. "Letters from the Island of St. Helena, exposing the unnecessary severity exercised towards Napoleon." London, 1818. 8vo.

5. "Mémoires de E. A. D. Comte de Las Casas."[1] Bruxelles, 1818. 8vo.

6. "Facts illustrative of the Treatment of Napoleon Bonaparte." By T. E. H. [Theodore Hook.] London, 1819. 8vo.

7. "An Exposition of some of the Transactions that have taken place at St. Helena since the appointment of Sir Hudson Lowe as Governor of that Island." By B. E. O'Meara. London, 1819. 8vo.

---

[1] So spelt in the titles of his books.

8. "Napoleon in Exile: or, A Voice from St. Helena."
By Barry E. O'Meara, Esq., his late Surgeon. 2 vols.
London, 1822. 8vo.

9. "Mémorial de Ste.-Hélène: Journal de la vie privée et
des conversations de l'Empereur Napoléon à Ste.-
Hélène." Par le Comte de Las Casas. 4 tom.
Londres, 1823. 8vo.

10. "Derniers Momens de Napoléon." Par C. F. Antommarchi. 2 tom. Paris et Londres, 1825. 8vo.

11. "Events of a Military Life." By Walter Henry, Surgeon
to the Forces. 2nd ed. 2 vols. London, 1843. sm.
8vo. [Vol. ii. pp. 1-97 have reference to St. Helena.]

12. "United Service Magazine." Oct. and Nov., 1843.
["Recollections of St. Helena," by Lieut.-Col. Basil
Jackson.] March, 1844. ["A Tribute to the Memory
of Sir Hudson Lowe," by the same.]

13. "Recollections of the Emperor Napoleon during the
first three years of his captivity on the island of St.
Helena." By L. E. Abell.[1] London, 1844. 12mo.

14. "History of Napoleon at St. Helena." By C. J. F. T.
de Montholon, Marquis de Montholon-Sémonville.
4 vols. London, 1846. 8vo.

15. "Récits de la Captivité de l'Empereur Napoléon à
Ste.-Hélène." By the same. 2 tom. Paris, 1847.
8vo.[2]

16. Third edition of Mrs. Abell's book, revised and added
to by Mrs. C. Johnston. London, 1873. 8vo.

17. "Berichte aus St. Helena zur Internirung Napoleon
Bonapartes. 1816-1818." Von B. v. Stürmer, herausg.
H. Schlitter. Wien, 1886. la. 8vo.

18. "Napoleon at St. Helena." By Barry Edward O'Meara,

---

[1] Mrs. Abell, formerly Miss Elizabeth Balcombe.

[2] For the differences between the English and the French
books by Montholon see "Quarterly Review," March, 1848.

his late Surgeon. 2 vols. London, 1888. 8vo. [A reprint of the "Voice from St. Helena," with certain additions and omissions.]

19. "The Century Magazine." Oct. and Nov., 1893. ["Taking Napoleon to St. Helena," from the diary of J. R. Glover, secretary to Admiral Cockburn.[1]]

20. "La Captivité de Ste.-Hélène d'après les rapports inédits du Marquis de Montchenu." Par Georges Firmin-Didot. Paris, 1894. 8vo.

21. "Revue Bleue." May-June, 1897. [" Le Prisonnier de Ste.-Hélène." The official reports of Count Balmain.]

22. "A Diary of St. Helena, 1816, 1817, the Journal of Lady Malcolm, containing the conversations of Napoleon with Sir Pulteney Malcolm." Edited by Sir Arthur Wilson. London, 1899. 8vo.

23. "Journal inédit de Sainte-Hélène, 1815-1818." Par le baron Gourgaud. 2 tom. Paris [1899]. 8vo.

24. "The Century Magazine." Feb.-April, 1900. [O'Meara's original diary.]

25. "Monthly Review." Jan., 1901. ["Colonel Wilks and Napoleon," by Julian S. Corbett.[2]]

26. "The Cornhill Magazine." Jan. and Feb., 1901. [Extracts from Letters and Journal of Sir G. Bingham, Lady Bingham, and others.[3]]

27. "Souvenirs de Ste.-Hélène par la Comtesse de Montholon, 1815-1816." Ed. par le Comte Fleury. Paris, 1901. 8vo.

28. "The English Historical Review." July, 1901. [Letters

---

[1] This was published together with Sir T. Ussher's narrative of the deportation to Elba in one vol. called "Napoleon's Last Voyages," 1895.

[2] Subsequently published separately by Mr. Murray.

[3] Part of this material was published in "Blackwood's Magazine," October, 1896.

of Lowe, Gneisenau, and others.] April, 1902. [Lowe's account of Napoleon's funeral.]

29. "With Napoleon at St. Helena, being the memoirs of Dr. John Stokoe, naval surgeon." Translated from the French of P. Frémeaux by Edith S. Stokoe. London, 1902. 8vo.

30. "Notes and Reminiscences of a Staff Officer, chiefly relating to the Waterloo Campaign and to St. Helena matters during the Captivity of Napoleon." By Lieut.-Colonel Basil Jackson. Ed. by R. C. Seaton. London, 1903. 8vo.[1]

SECONDARY SOURCES

31. "Quarterly Review." Nos. 31 (Oct., 1816), 32 (Jan. 1817), 34 (July, 1817), 55 (Oct., 1822), 65 (Dec., 1825), 164 (March, 1848).

32. "Edinburgh Review." Nos. 59 (Dec., 1816), 73 (June 1822), 76 (May, 1823).

33. "Life of Napoleon Bonaparte." by Sir Walter Scott. 9 vols. London, 1827. 8vo.

34. "United Service Magazine." April-June, 1844. [Memoir of Sir Hudson Lowe.]

35. "History of the Captivity of Napoleon at St. Helena; from the Letters and Journals of the late Lieut.-General Sir Hudson Lowe, and Official Documents not before made public." By William Forsyth, M.A. 3 vols. London, 1853. 8vo.

36. "Revue des Deux Mondes." 1855, vol. ix. pp. 292-339. [Criticism of Forsyth's book.]

37. "Napoleon I." Von Dr. August Fournier. 1889. 8vo. [Part of the series "Das Wissen der Gegenwart."]

38. "Sir Hudson Lowe and Napoleon." By R. C. Seaton. London, 1898. 8vo.

[1] This book was originally printed for private circulation in 1877.

39. "Napoleon: the Last Phase." By Lord Rosebery. London, 1900. roy. 8vo.

40. "Napoleon: Extracts from the *Times* and *Morning Chronicle*, 1815-1821, relating to Napoleon's life at St. Helena." London, 1901. 8vo.

41. "Napoleon auf St. Helena." Von Dr. Edm. Meyer. 1902. [A part of "Napoleon I.," edited by Dr. J. von Pflugk-Harttung.]

42. "Life of Napoleon I." 2 vols. By Dr. J. Holland Rose. London, 1902. 8vo.

43. "Napoleon's Tod im Spiegel der zeitgenössischen Presse und Dichtung." Von Paul Holzhausen. Frankfurt a. Main, 1902. 8vo.

44. "Owens College Historical Essays." London, 1902. 8vo. ["Napoleon's Detention at St. Helena," by Dr. J. Holland Rose.]

45. "Napoleon. A Sketch of his Life, Character, Struggles and Achievements." By Thomas E. Watson. New York, 1902. 8vo.

46. "La Leggenda Napoleonica." Licurgo Cappelletti. Torino, 1903. 8vo.

47. "St. Helena: the Historic Island." By E. L. Jackson. London, 1903. 8vo.

INDEX

AJACCIO, Lowe at, 39-41.
Alexander, Emperor of
Russia, receives Lowe in au-
dience, 56; confers order on
Lowe, 61; instructions to Bal-
main, 138 n.; interview with
Countess Balmain, 143; death,
239.

Alison, "History of Europe,"
quoted, 58 n., 190 and n.

"American Cyclopaedia," quoted, 67 n., App. A.

Amherst, Lord, at St. Helena,
120.

Antommarchi, Dr., arrival at St.
Helena, 199; his book, 113,
190.

Balmain, Count, Russian Commissioner, 135; his instructions, 137-138; on Montholon,
92 n.; opinion of Lowe, 144-
145, 246; description of St.
Helena, 173-175; his reports
quoted, 20, 103, 106 n., 192,
204.

Balmain, Countess, marriage of,
143; meets the Emperor Alexander, 143.

Bathurst, Lord, instructions to
Lowe, 156; letters to Lowe,
118, 166, 168, 229; on the
foreign Commissioners, 135,
138; urges new precautions,
181; speech in the House of
Lords on the treatment of
Napoleon, 165, 169-170; on
the bust of Napoleon's son,
215; on presents to Napoleon
generally, 220; urges Lowe
to write in his own defence,
233, 236; offers Lowe the
government of Antigua, 238.

Bautzen, battle of, 57.

Baxter, Dr., on the monopoly
of the Longwood contractors,
202; on the alleged fictitious
bulletins, 209.

Beatson, General Alexander, on
St. Helena as a place of exile,
80, 171 n.

Bernadotte, Prince Royal of
Sweden, conversation of Lowe
with, 55-56.

Berthier, General, letter of remonstrance to, from Lowe, 47,
225.

Bertrand, Count, character and

CHISWICK PRESS: CHARLES WHITTINGHAM AND CO.
TOOKS COURT, CHANCERY LANE, LONDON.

Lightning Source UK Ltd.
Milton Keynes UK
11 July 2010

156838UK00001B/20/P